A WHITE LIBERAL COLLEGE

PRESIDENT IN

THE JIM CROW SOUTH

MERCER UNIVERSITY PRESS

Endowed by

TOM WATSON BROWN
and
THE WATSON-BROWN FOUNDATION, INC.

A WHITE LIBERAL COLLEGE PRESIDENT IN

THE JIM CROW SOUTH

*Guy Herbert Wells and the YWCA at Georgia
State College for Women, 1934–1953*

Sandra E. Godwin

with Helen Matthews Lewis

MERCER UNIVERSITY PRESS

Macon, Georgia

2021

MUP / H1006

© 2021 by Mercer University Press
Published by Mercer University Press
1501 Mercer University Drive
Macon, Georgia 31207
All rights reserved

25 24 23 22 21   5 4 3 2 1

Books published by Mercer University Press are printed on acid-free
paper that meets the requirements of the American National Standard for
Information Sciences—Permanence of Paper for Printed Library
Materials.

Printed and bound in Canada.

This book is set in Adobe Caslon Pro.

Cover/jacket design by Burt&Burt.

ISBN   978-0-88146-790-1
Cataloging-in-Publication Data is available from the Library of Congress

For my late mother,
Peggy Gail Scott Godwin (1935–2014).

Contents

Preface

I became interested in the Young Women's Christian Association (YWCA) through my friendship with Helen Matthews Lewis.[1] I met her in 2005 when she received an alumni award at Georgia College & State University (Georgia College), where I currently teach. In 1946, Lewis graduated from Georgia State College for Women (GSCW), as Georgia College was then called.[2] At GSCW, Lewis was a social science major and a member of the campus chapter of the YWCA. She participated in the YWCA-sponsored Religious Emphasis Week, among other events and activities, where she heard guest speakers—progressive Southerners—who changed her way of thinking about race and religion. Her "Aha!" moment was when she heard Baptist preacher and Koinonia Farm founder, Clarence Jordan, tell his version of "The Good Samaritan." The Good Samaritan turned out to be an elderly black man who helped people in need as he traveled down the road, while the white clergy passed them by. At that moment, Lewis said to herself, "This is what religion is all about."

Lewis went on to earn a master's degree from the University of Virginia in 1949. She explained that she "had read *The [sic] American Dilemma* at GSCW, and, inspired and educated by my suffragette teachers and the YWCA and social science faculty at GSCW," she wrote a master's thesis titled, "The Woman's Movement and the Negro Movement—Parallel Struggles for

---

[1] Matthews was Helen's last name while a student at Georgia State College for Women. She is referenced as "Lewis" throughout the book.

[2] See Appendix I for other names of the college and associated dates.

Rights."[3] Lewis was awarded a PhD in sociology from the University of Kentucky and afterwards worked with coal mining communities and families in Appalachia. Central themes of her work have been how religion and culture in Appalachian communities are sources of empowerment and how women play major roles in their communities—whether they are organizing against the coal industry or working for sustainable community development. This central theme of Lewis's work helped establish the area of Appalachian Studies. As she traveled the world as a well-known Appalachian scholar and activist, people often asked how she came to commit herself to the region and its people. She explained that her commitment stemmed from her "radicalization" at a small women's college in Georgia. "No one believes me when I say that," she told me, and this is what made her want to write a book about the YWCA.

When I met her, Lewis asked if I knew any graduate students who might want to help her with the book. Luckily I didn't know of any graduate students, because I wanted to help. She and I began working on the book in 2005. In the beginning, both of us were writers and archival researchers but, as it turns out, I have written the book and Lewis's contribution has been as occasional editor, archival researcher, and a promoter of the story.

As I researched the archive at Georgia College and shared my findings with Lewis, we realized that the book was more about the college president Guy Herbert Wells than it was about the YWCA. However, we would not have a story about President Wells without the YWCA. The student YWCA was ahead of its time in that it created integrated spaces where black and white college students came together as equals, and in those spaces white women began to acknowledge and critique their racial

---

[3] Lewis, "GSCW in the 1940s," 54.

privilege. This book is about how the YWCA's commitment to a critique of the status quo was the major catalyst for President Wells's learning to play the middle. The women of the GSCW YWCA who functioned as catalysts were part of a small, inter-collegiate, interracial movement that helped move Southerners, particularly white Southerners, beyond what they had learned about race and the social order.

Acknowledgments

Many people—colleagues, acquaintances, friends, and family—have contributed to the writing of this book. My dear friend and colleague Beauty Bragg read chapter drafts and gently guided me on how to bring to the surface what I was trying to say. Beauty and I formed a writing group at Georgia College with Esther Lopez, Katie Simon, and the late Mark Vail, all of whom provided support and encouragement. Professional editor Leila Weinstein also provided invaluable feedback over several weekends in North Carolina. Jacquelyn Dowd Hall and the late John Egerton read early drafts and let us know the book was worth writing. Thanks also go to the late Tina Yarborough, Ainsley Eubanks, and Valerie Aranda from the Georgia College art department who read early work, and to Emily Gomez, who offered support and her photographic expertise.

Archivists as well as readers deserve all my gratitude. I learned about the great care archivists take to maintain historical records and that they expect visitors to demonstrate that same care and respect. All archivists I worked with patiently ushered me into their world. The archivists at Georgia College Special Collections, at the Ina Dillard Russell Library, were patient, knowledgeable, and fun to be around. I enjoyed many conversations with Nancy Davis Bray about GSCW history. Other archivists and special collections staff at Georgia College have moved to other positions, but I thank all of them: Joshua Kitchens, Chris Ellis, and Kate Pope. Joshua was especially helpful with a bibliography for Jane Cassels. Jessica McQuain's help was also invaluable. She located the images and put them in the proper format. I cannot say enough about Maida Goodwin, a former archivist at the Sophia Smith Collection of Women's History at Smith

College. Not only did she never tire of my questions about the YWCA, the more intricate they were, the more eager she was to answer them. Taronda Spencer, former archivist at Spelman College Collections, had extensive knowledge about the YWCA at Spelman and did all she could to provide me with materials I could access from home. Other archivists whose help was much appreciated are: Marianne Bradley at Agnes Scott College, Debbie Thompson at Brenau University, Stacey L. Wright at Valdosta State, and Sybil McNeil at Wesleyan College.

I would also like to thank interviewees Catherine Leathers Hartley, the late Elizabeth Shreve Ryan, Marion Denoni Barber, the late Emily Cottingham Stuart, Bob Stuart, Joan Browning, and Dorothy Leland for the time they gave out of their busy lives. In many cases, these individuals opened their homes to both Helen and me. (All interviews conducted for this book were approved by the Georgia College & State University Institutional Review Board on September 19, 2008.) Special thanks go to Joan Browning. She was a GSCW student and a freedom rider and graciously shared her files and her broad and impressive knowledge about civil rights history.

Joan is an independent scholar and historian, and I have learned much from her and other historians. Although I am not a historian, Joan invited me to speak about the book on panels with her at two history conferences. I learned from Joan and her colleague Catherine Oglesby that I was not alone and that all historians struggle to tell a story. Joan also introduced me to historian Patricia Sullivan, who offered helpful strategies for writing a historical narrative. Historian Delma Presley taught me a lot about Guy Wells and unknowingly gave me the narrative structure for this book; I'm just sorry it took me so long to realize it. I owe special gratitude to historian Frances Sanders Taylor Anton. Her dissertation, to my knowledge, is the only study about the

Southern student YWCA during the early civil rights era. Frances generously shared all her files with us, including her interview with the late Mary "Polly" Moss Cuthbertson. What a treasure trove!

I also want to express my utmost gratitude to Helen Matthews Lewis, who had the idea that brought us together. From the weekend in Morganton, Georgia, in August of 2005, we have come a long way, and all throughout, Helen has been the book's best promoter. She has become my friend and has included me in her own circle of friends. A special thanks to her friend and coauthor on *Mountain Sisters*, Monica Appleby, who had faith all along the way. I also want to thank Helen's friend Darlene, who helped with library research. I am grateful to Georgia College for financial support especially that of Dr. Eric Tenbus, dean of the College of Arts & Sciences; Dr. Carolyn Denard, chief diversity officer of the Office of Inclusive Excellence; and Dr. Costas Spirou, provost. Provost Spirou also provided dependable advice and moral support.

And, of course, I am grateful to Mercer University Press for publishing the book and to director Marc Jolley and publishing assistant Marsha Luttrell for their patience and wise guidance. I also appreciate the copyeditor's thorough commentary, on-the-mark suggestions, and thoughtful tone.

I thank my soul mates from grad school, Katie Hyde and Francine Byrne, who inspired me from day one. They reassured me and expressed confidence in my ability when I doubted it myself. I am also grateful for my mentor, the late Mary Rogers, who in 1989 saw in me a potential sociologist. I took her course at the University of West Florida quite by chance (at the time I was more interested in psychology). Yet her brilliance and uncompromising sense of justice changed my worldview and the course of my life.

More thanks go to all my family, but a special few provided extra support. My nephew Aaron Godwin opened his home to me on my frequent library trips to Atlanta and always lifted my spirits. His friend Clint Beardon, Clint's mother, Barbara, and his late great-aunt Dora also deserve thanks. Clint's aunt graduated from GSCW, and soon after we discovered this, Barbara happily drove me to Rome to interview her.

I would also like to thank my father, Terrell Wayne Godwin, whose favorite question has been, "How's the book coming?" I appreciate his interest and how the struggles of academic publishing gave us a lot to talk about. I thank my sisters, Suzette Godwin and Stephanie Solomon. Suzi provided comic relief, and Stephanie read an early draft of the entire manuscript. She patiently listened to my detailed analysis of why and how I would get stuck and why and how I could (or could not) push through. She never, ever tired of listening, and there was no one who understood better.

More than anyone else, I thank my late mother, Peggy Gail Scott Godwin, for giving me life and love and for encouraging me to stay in college when I wanted to drop out after my first semester. I thank her for the unwavering faith she had in me.

—Sandra Elizabeth Godwin
Milledgeville, June 2020

Abbreviations

A&M:	Agricultural and Mechanical Arts
BOR:	Board of Regents
CCRA:	Coordinated Council of Religious Activities
CIC:	Commission on Interracial Cooperation
GC:	Georgia College
GN&IC:	Georgia Normal & Industrial College
GSCW:	Georgia State College for Women
GSWC:	Georgia State Woman's College
GTC:	Georgia Teachers College
NAACP:	National Association for the Advancement of Colored People
N&I:	Normal and Industrial School
SACSS:	Southern Association of Colleges and Secondary Schools
SCHW:	Southern Conference for Human Welfare
SGTC:	South Georgia Teachers College
SNCC:	Student Nonviolent Coordinating Committee
UGA:	University of Georgia
USG:	University System of Georgia
WAVES:	Women Appointed for Voluntary Emergency Service
WCG:	The Woman's College of Georgia
YMCA:	Young Men's Christian Association
YWCA:	Young Women's Christian Association

Chapter 1

Introduction:
Higher Education in Georgia:
A Site of Early Civil Rights Struggle and
Learning to Play the Middle

"He [President Wells] was a consummate Southern politician, a liberal who knows how to live in a world of conservatives on race."
                              —Historian Delma Eugene Presley[1]

This book is about the political nature of higher education, specifically the position of a college or university president. It documents how one president of a public institution of higher education in Georgia responded to a student organization's race reform efforts during the early civil rights era. Through the lens of the campus YWCA we learn: (1) how higher education was a major site of civil rights struggle and (2) how and why one president learned to negotiate a middle political position between the white supremacist state and a racially progressive student organization. The book thus serves as a resource for scholars of higher education interested in the role of college presidents in

---

[1] Delma Eugene Presley (Georgia Southern professor emeritus and museum director emeritus), in discussion with author, June 18, 2008, transcript in author's possession.

civil rights struggle. The book will also be of interest to those who want to know more about the YWCA.

Guy Herbert Wells drives the narrative as a white liberal who served as president of the all-white Georgia State College for Women, in Milledgeville, Georgia. We tell of President Wells's inner turmoil as he tried to stay true to his own liberal values on race while working for governors opposed to civil rights reform. These conditions constituted the crucible within which he learned to survive by playing the middle.

Historian of higher education Eddie R. Cole argued that historians have paid scant attention to the role of college presidents in the civil rights movement of the 1960s. They occasionally detail college presidents' response to students' race activism at predominantly black universities in the Southeastern United States, but even then, presidents are most often an afterthought. For example, in historian Joy Williamson's powerful 2008 examination of black colleges in Mississippi, *Radicalizing the Ebony Tower*, she focused on students and faculty. She occasionally identified college presidents who had limited power and sought to play the middle between students and faculty who advocated for change and state-level administrators and governors who supported the status quo, but her focus was students and, to a lesser extent, faculty.

In contrast, Cole featured Franklin D. Murphy, the white chancellor (or president) of the University of California-Los Angeles (UCLA) and his relationship with a campus chapter of the Student Nonviolent Coordinating Committee (SNCC). He wrote of Murphy's effort to make UCLA more inclusive, but the reality was that black students at UCLA and in the city of Los Angeles faced exclusion. Cole proposed that understanding the history of how college presidents in the United States have responded to black student protest helps us gain a better understanding of the relationship between the power of the state, the power of the institution manifested in the position of president, and the power of students. A historical perspective, he argued, provides crucial insight into contemporary black student protest on campuses across the country, and it allows us to acknowledge a continuing civil rights struggle in higher education despite significant gains. Cole argued that we should acknowledge the "tension between the image of inclusion at U.S. colleges and universities and several students' lived realities with racism on campuses."[2]

Presidential biographies offer another angle on the role of university presidents in civil rights struggle. In his 1994 biography of Rufus B. Atwood, president of Kentucky State College (previously Kentucky State College for Negroes) from 1929 to 1962, historian Gerald L. Smith also examined the difficulty of a college president's negotiation of a political middle ground. As a biographer, he told Atwood's life story, but he also revealed the president's struggle to manage the tension between satisfying his student body on the one hand and state elected officials on the other. Smith identified several black college presidents during the early civil rights era at both public and private institutions who agonized over managing this same tension: Frederick Patterson, president of Tuskegee Institute; Benner C. Turner, president of South Carolina State College; H. Council Trenholm, president of Alabama State College; and F. D. Bluford, president of North Carolina Agricultural and Technical College. Smith argued that scholars of African American history have neglected the role college presidents have played in civil rights struggles. Another comparable study of a black college president is the 2003 biography of Charles S. Johnson, Fisk

---

[2] Cole, "College Presidents and Black Student Protests," 87.

University's first black president, who served from 1946 until his death in 1956. Gilpin and Gasman also explore this tension at certain points in Johnson's career.

Warren Ashby's 1980 biography, *Frank Porter Graham: A Southern Liberal*, is another comparable biography in that Ashby explored a similar tension between the state and a university president. As a white liberal president, however, Graham's struggle was decidedly different from Atwood's. As president of the University of North Carolina at Chapel Hill (1930–1949), Graham received strong public criticism for allowing the campus Young Men's Christian Association (YMCA) and a sociology professor to invite African American poet Langston Hughes to speak on campus. He also took heat for allowing British philosopher Bertrand Russell to speak. The president's office was inundated with letters of complaint, and President Graham responded to every letter writer in detail. Ashby described this experience for Graham as a battle that left scars.[3]

Although our book is not a biography, we explore in depth how President Wells negotiated a middle ground. Our analysis of presidential correspondence focuses on how the president of GSCW responded to a student organization that had garnered widespread negative attention, both nationally and regionally, as a "Negro-controlled" and communistic organization. We also explore how the politics of the state of Georgia shaped the president's response. We explore, as does Cole, the relationship between a president, the state, and a student organization. At many colleges and universities across the South during the 1920s, '30s, and '40s, the YWCA introduced white students to the small, intercollegiate, interracial movement. This caught the attention of state leaders who pressured President Wells to limit

---

[3] Ashby, *Frank Porter Graham*, 127.

4

and sometimes silence students' race reform efforts. In *A White Liberal College President*, we track the president's political moves to the left and to the right as he responded to the race reform efforts of the YWCA and the pressure from the white supremacist state.

This book examines the complexities of political ideology in the South during the 1930s and 1940s. In *Higher Education and the Civil Rights Movement*, historian Peter Wallenstein identified a trend in Southern politics that he labeled "a dual tradition of dissent." He noted that as weaknesses in white supremacy and challenges to economic oppression emerged during the civil rights era, many college presidents and other school administrators looked for "ways to accommodate the agents of change while appeasing the forces of resistance to change."[4] We apply Wallenstein's dual tradition to the presidency of Guy Herbert Wells, who served GSCW from 1934 to 1953. The student chapter of the YWCA and its progressive race reform is the lens through which we investigate and reveal this dual tradition. We describe this tradition as a back and forth between a supportive response to the campus YWCA that reflected a liberal position and a harmful response that reflected a conservative position. President Wells's vacillation between left and right positions created an overall impression as a moderate residing in the middle of the political spectrum as it existed in the era of Jim Crow segregation in Georgia. The campus YWCA, because of members' ability to push the racial boundaries of segregation, allows us to understand how a college president could navigate such a position. The president's ability to play the middle created space for progressive change and allowed the campus YWCA, in the short term, to function as a viable or-

---

[4] Wallenstein, *Higher Education and the Civil Rights Movement*, 4.

ganization despite strong criticism from judges, other college presidents, members of the state board of regents, other government officials, and prominent citizens. However, in the long term, playing the middle strengthened the institution's racist foundation. This book thus illustrates how higher education in Georgia was and is a site of civil rights struggle.

The space President Wells and others created for progressive change was small because of the powerful hold of white supremacy. All Georgia's governors during the time frame for this book—1934 to 1953—were committed to segregation: Richard B. Russell Jr., Eugene Talmadge, Eurith D. Rivers, Herman Talmadge, Melvin E. Thompson, and Ellis Arnall. As historian Charles Gurr explained, moderation, when it came to race,

> is a relative term in Georgia politics for much of the heart of the twentieth century. Sanford [chancellor of the University System of Georgia], like Gowen [a moderate legislator and candidate for governor]...and the better-known Ellis Arnall, was by today's litmus tests merely a moderate racist. Any of these gentlemen, and thousands more like them all over the country, were at best thoughtful and kind to blacks tête-à-tête. They were not coarse men, but beneath their manners were value systems planted firmly in the Georgia of the previous century.[5]

Journalist John Egerton spoke of this dynamic as "the peculiar Southern panorama of liberalism."[6] Ellis Arnall is a good illustration of one dimension of this peculiar panorama. Even though he was by far Georgia's most progressive governor at the time, during his campaign he expressed his commitment to segregation: "I am a white man," he told an audience in Ringgold, Georgia, "and I am ready to defend with my blood the Consti-

---

[5] Gurr, *The Personal Equation*, 159.
[6] Egerton, *Speak Now Against the Day*, 289.

tution of Georgia which provides for a separation of races."[7] The racial order, promised Arnall, would remain unchanged under his watch. The commitment to segregation, and thus racism, at the level of state policy and governance is the backdrop for our exploration of President Wells's enactment of a "dual tradition." His own commitment to segregation served as yet another dimension of the peculiar panorama of liberalism among Southern whites.

President Guy Herbert Wells

Delma Presley, a retired Georgia Southern University historian, saw President Wells as a leader of "great strength, great ability." Presley thought Wells would have made a powerful chancellor, mainly because "he believed in education...because it had meant so much to *him* and...he was truly inspired by the stories of young people who [lived on] farms and came to college and became great educators or doctors or lawyers. He kept up with them. He was really proud of them. He believed in education."[8] Presley chronicled the founding and growth of Georgia Southern.[9] Georgia Southern was once known as South Georgia Teachers College (SGTC), where Wells served as president before becoming president at GSCW.

President Wells's colleagues also regarded him highly as a leader. James C. Bonner, a former historian at Georgia College and coauthor of *A Centennial History of Georgia College*, said of President Wells: "He had the peculiar ability to understand how a college worked, and he had great powers of discernment."[10]

---

[7] Novotny, *This Georgia Rising*, 264n111.

[8] Presley, discussion.

[9] Delma Eugene Presley, *The Southern Century: Georgia Southern University: 1906–2006* (Statesboro: Georgia Southern University, 2006).

[10] Hair et al., *A Centennial History*, 171.

Georgia College's former dean of instruction Donald MacMahon said of President Wells: "Of all the educators I ever met, as far as greatness of human spirit is concerned, Dr. Wells would rank first."[11] The late John H. Lounsbury, who was dean emeritus of the John H. Lounsbury College of Education at Georgia College, met President Wells and remarked on his concern for students: "I was impressed with Guy Wells, mainly because he was so student-centered. [He] met with students informally for conversations."[12] Robert (Bob) Wilson, professor emeritus of history at Georgia College, the university historian, and also a coauthor of *A Centennial History*, identified President Wells as one of the three best past presidents of Georgia College.[13]

President Wells was born in Georgia, educated almost entirely in Georgia, and acquired all of his professional training in Georgia. He was born on September 26, 1892, in Temple, in Carroll County, in the northwestern part of the state, and grew up on a farm. After high school, he attended Mercer University in Macon and graduated with a BA in 1915. He later took a job as superintendent of the Dodge County School District in Eastman, Georgia, and earned a master's degree from Columbia University in 1925. He completed one year of postgraduate work at Peabody College in Nashville but never earned a PhD. He was awarded an honorary LLD from Mercer in 1934 and was often referred to as "Dr. Wells."[14] President Wells described his values as a leader in higher education at his first talk at GSCW: "I am not a scholar myself but I am able to appreciate a

---

[11] Ibid., 171–72.

[12] John H. Lounsbury (dean emeritus of the John H. Lounsbury College of Education at Georgia College) in discussion with author, June 27, 2018.

[13] Bob Wilson, email message to author, June 14, 2020.

[14] Hair et al., *A Centennial History*, 172.

person who is one. But I think character is greater than scholarship. Building love, honesty, and loyalty into one's life is essential."[15]

President Wells was active in Milledgeville organizations. He was a member of the Democratic Party, the Chamber of Commerce, the Kiwanis Club, and the Rotary Club, and he was a Mason and a deacon in the First Baptist Church. Wells approached life with a sense of humor, and at local speaking events was known to tell off-color jokes. In his first talk on campus, he said, "I appreciate fun and humor; life would be stale without either."[16]

Guy Wells's sense of humor gave him a reputation for lacking a bit in social graces. GSCW professor of psychology Frances Ross Hicks described him, in his early years at GSCW, as a "diamond in the rough."[17] Emily Cottingham, YWCA leader in the 1940s at GSCW, who is featured in chapter 5, often shared a Sunday meal with the president and his family. She recalled how President Wells fed his pets from the table: "He and his wife had me over for Sunday dinner a lot of the time. He would feed the dog or the cat from the table and students would say, Oooh. How uncouth! And I'd say that was just a friendly thing for him to do. But I loved it!"[18] Cottingham found President Wells's lack of refinement endearing, as did many GSCW students, faculty, staff, and people of Milledgeville.

---

[15] "President Elect Visits College," *The Colonnade* (April 24, 1934): 1. University Archives, Special Collections, Ina Dillard Russell Library, Georgia College, Milledgeville, GA (hereafter cited as *The Colonnade*).

[16] Ibid.

[17] Hair et al., *A Centennial History*, 172.

[18] Emily Cottingham Stuart (YWCA resident secretary at GSCW, 1943–1947), in discussion with author and Helen Matthews Lewis, Blacksburg, VA, December 17, 2007; transcript in author's possession.

President Wells was a big man, occasionally awkward, and a lover of trees. William Ivy Hair, also a former historian at Georgia College and coauthor of *A Centennial History*, described him as "stout and jowly" with "nervous energy [that] led him to pace ahead of people he was talking to, and chew unlit cigars to fragments."[19] Perhaps to calm his nervous energy, he wanted a campus filled with shady oaks and flowering trees. At SGTC he had dogwoods and crepe myrtles planted. At GSCW he had oak trees planted in the central area, most of which survive today. In his effort to beautify campus, President Wells also restored old buildings and built new ones, such as Beeson and Sanford halls, and had the Baldwin County Jail removed, which was located only a few feet from Bell dormitory.[20]

Perhaps one of the most telling indicators of President Wells as an educator was how he responded to Cottingham's revelation that she questioned her own religious beliefs. President Wells interviewed Cottingham for the full-time resident secretary position for the campus YWCA in 1943. The resident secretary was a director of the organization and was required to live on campus during the academic year as well as during one summer session. Cottingham reported that President Wells assured her that her questioning spirit—"I still don't know what I believe about God," she told him—was exactly what he wanted in a resident secretary. She recalled President Wells's response:

> "What I *really* want is somebody who's not going to tell these girls what they have to believe." He said a lot of them come from poor working families. "A lot of them come from Baptist families, and they think that dancing is a sin, being happy is a sin, and that's *not* what I want these girls to come out of here believing. The more you can help them

---

[19] Hair et al., *A Centennial History*, 172.
[20] Ibid., 190–91.

think through what *they* find out about God and what *they* want to believe, and if they can't even believe in God, so be it."[21]

After this discussion President Wells hired Cottingham as the next YWCA resident secretary. She is one of the three secretaries featured.

In 1943, the year President Wells hired Emily Cottingham, famous Southern writer Mary Flannery O'Connor had been a student at GSCW for one year. During her three years at GSCW, like most GSCW students, she did not participate in the race reform efforts of the YWCA. Her friend and GSCW graduate Elizabeth Shreve Ryan (1946) described O'Connor as "apolitical."[22] In contrast, Lewis suggested that O'Connor was indeed political; she was just quiet about it. O'Connor and Lewis worked together on the 1945 issue of *The Spectrum*, the student yearbook, and Lewis described O'Connor as

> an observer and critic more than a participant in most of the college activities. Her writings and cartoons were those of an objective observer who reported the campus activities with great wit, creativity, and ridicule....She used her cartoons and satirical writings as a form of rebellion or resistance.... She could draw cartoons of YWCA girls holding candles, but I don't think she ever had cartoons of nuns or priests or Catholic rituals or celebrations.[23]

For the most part, O'Connor saw GSCW as an inferior institution. Lewis noted that she "abhorred progressive, modern, secular education and wanted more classics, and she felt most of her classes inadequate and her education sadly lacking." Lewis's experience of GSCW was entirely different. She praised the

---

[21] Cottingham Stuart, discussion.
[22] Lewis, "GSCW in the 1940s," 56.
[23] Ibid., 56–57.

YWCA and most of her professors and saw GSCW as the place where she was "radicalized" and inspired to work for racial and economic justice. For Lewis and a small number of students, the YWCA at GSCW served as their introduction to matters of social justice.

Organization of the Book

Chapter 2 describes the two events that set the stage for President Wells's political education: his transfer from South Georgia Teachers College to Georgia State College for Women and the race reform work of the student YWCA. The chapter discusses President Wells's successes at SGTC and his involuntary transfer in the context of the creation of the University System of Georgia (USG). Working under this new system meant that President Wells had the governor and a new board to answer to. The chapter speculates as to whether or not President Wells's liberal values on race had anything to do with the transfer. Chapter 2 also introduces GSCW and the YWCA and its race reform agenda.

Chapter 3 features President Wells's first lesson: keep a close watch on the YWCA. It highlights the student gathering that caused him the most trouble: a YWCA-sponsored visit to Fort Valley Normal & Industrial (N&I) School, a black coed institution about an hour's drive from Milledgeville. The chapter identifies key people who were supporters and strong critics of the trip and introduces the YWCA resident secretary, Mary "Polly" Moss, who planned the trip. The chapter chronicles the consequences of the visit for Moss and President Wells and provides a discussion of how all across the South an effort to link civil rights and Communism worked to the YWCA's and thus President Wells's disadvantage. It begins an analysis of gender that is continued in chapter 4, namely that gender is

12

fundamentally connected to the suppression of race reform by the control of women's sexuality. The chapter also details President Wells's dwindling support of the YWCA as criticism of their interracial activities became more public.

Chapter 4, more than any other chapter, shows how President Wells adapted to his new surroundings. Once he understood that the YWCA and its progressive women could cause trouble for him, he learned to provide uneven support to the organization to keep its members under control. This was his second lesson. The pattern of uneven support that began soon after the trip to Fort Valley was solidified in the events covered in chapter 4. From mid-1936 through 1938, President Wells allowed liberal and radical speakers on campus, but by 1939, he had banned all students from all interracial gatherings. His interrogation of students who attended interracial gatherings, his search for a moderate resident secretary, and his hiring of a well-known liberal professor also revealed his middle position on and uneven support for the YWCA. Another example of uneven support was to suggest to the chancellor that the name "YWCA" be changed to "Religious Activities." President James Ross McCain of Agnes Scott College (1923–1951), a private women's college associated with the Presbyterian Church in Decatur, Georgia, faced challenges similar to those faced by President Wells. For example, President McCain also suggested a name change for the campus YWCA at Agnes Scott. The young women of the YWCA at both Agnes Scott and GSCW were surveilled by many white supremacists in the South. Chapter 4 thus continues an analysis of gender with a discussion of the cult of white Southern womanhood and whites' fear of miscegenation.

Chapter 5 focuses on President Wells's third lesson, that it was safe to move left when a liberal governor was in office.

Chapter 5 investigates the sometimes-chaotic forces of progressive change in the state of Georgia in the 1940s. It discusses the Cocking-Pittman controversy that overshadowed the USG and created a strong critique of the leadership of Governor Eugene Talmadge. Ellis Arnall defeated Talmadge, and the chapter details some of the progressive legislative changes that came about under his leadership. This allowed President Wells to take a more relaxed approach to overseeing the YWCA. This more relaxed approach is exemplified through his relationship with resident secretary Emily Cottingham. World War II is also discussed as a force of progressive change. The chapter concludes with an analysis of President Wells's success thus far at playing the middle.

Chapter 6 reveals President Wells's fourth and final lesson: stay left when it's safe. The chapter proposes several reasons for President Wells's comfort with maintaining a left political position: growing public support for race reform, YWCA decline, and his own impending retirement. The chapter features Ku Klux Klan activity in and around Milledgeville and strong public critique of the cross-burnings, one of which occurred in front of the Old Governor's Mansion where President and Ruby Wells resided. President Wells received widespread praise for condemning the cross-burning, which emboldened him to stay on the course he began while Ellis Arnall was governor. The chapter traces President Wells's continued flexible approach to managing the YWCA during this relatively progressive period in Georgia and details the YWCA's decline at local, regional, and national levels. The chapter concludes with a discussion of President Wells's search for work abroad and his retirement.

The conclusion, chapter 7, proposes that little has changed at Georgia College since President Wells's tenure, in that it is a predominantly white institution. The chapter compares President Wells's inner turmoil from playing the middle with Dorothy Leland, who served as president of Georgia College from 2004 to 2011. It proposes that primarily because of its lack of racial diversity, Georgia College remains a site of civil rights struggle. The chapter engages with freedom-of-speech debates in higher education as understood by President Leland and her experience at both Georgia College and University of California-Merced, the institution she led after leaving Georgia College. And it identifies the lack of such a debate during President Wells's tenure. The book ends by discussing the costs and benefits of President Wells's middle-of-the-road strategies and reflects on the role of broad-based social movements in creating systemic change in social institutions such as criminal justice (as the result of current protests led by Black Lives Matter) and higher education.

Chapter 2

Setting the Stage:
President Wells's Transfer to
GSCW and the YWCA

The Great Depression led to the centralization of power that created the University System of Georgia (USG). This was the system under which President Wells was transferred from South Georgia Teachers College to Georgia State College for Women. Under the cheaper and more efficient system, President Wells acquired superiors whose political positions had to be taken into account as he led GSCW. At GSCW, YWCA students pushed racial boundaries in ways that YWCA students at SGTC had not. These conditions set the stage for President Wells to play the middle. In this new system he could be ousted if he did not maintain control over students in a way that pleased his new superiors in the capitol. This differed from the earlier days of higher education institutions in Georgia when presidents and local leaders had more decision-making power.

Prior to 1932, when the USG went into effect, there was a proliferation of educational institutions administered by local leaders. Historian Roger Geiger noted that in the United States college enrollments doubled between 1914 and 1924, largely because of the increase in high school graduates. And the increase in high school graduates stemmed from the growing availability of high schools, particularly in rural areas.[1] Elected officials across the country opted to use state money to provide a variety of opportunities for higher learning for the growing number of high school graduates, and in Georgia there was a wide array. Some institutions blended the last few years of high school with the first few years of college, as did Georgia Normal & Industrial College (GN&IC)/GSCW.[2] Also, in Georgia, agricultural and mechanical arts (A&M) schools were created to address high school needs for students in rural areas. Eight A&M district high schools were established in Georgia in 1907 and 1908 which by the mid-1920s were converted into colleges.[3] Local boards of trustees governed the institutions, and their establishment was based on local needs.

The Creation of the University System of Georgia

In the early twentieth century, local leaders governed the higher education institutions created in Georgia to address the growing number of high school graduates. That changed, largely as a result of the Great Depression. During this time Governor Richard B. Russell Jr. (1931–1933) saw a need to reduce state expenditures and create a more efficient system of authority in higher education. That need was met on January 1, 1932, when the USG went into effect. Governor Russell appointed eleven members to form a single board of regents to govern the system, one from each of the ten congressional districts and one member at-large.

The new board of regents appointed a team of educators and economists, all from outside the South, to conduct a survey

---

[1] Geiger, *The History of American Higher Education*, 429.

[2] See Appendix I for names of the college and presidents who have served.

[3] Fincher, *Historical Development*, 4–5.

18

to determine the needs of the system and how best to govern the institutions.[4] In 1933, the team concluded that the structure of the system was too political. They recommended that the governor not serve as an ex officio member of the board and that regents should not represent their congressional districts but should represent instead the state's "economic and cultural interests." The committee based their recommendations on guidelines from the National Association of State Universities. Committee members stated in their report that "the theory (of *ex officio* membership) is thoroughly unsound, the practice is even worse."[5] The new board of regents ignored the committee's recommendations and the governor continued to serve as the highest authority in the system with the power to appoint the board of regents, one from each congressional district and one at-large, as Governor Russell had originally authorized. These appointees were then to be approved by the state senate. In less than ten years, this political structure would prove to be severely detrimental to the accredited institutions that were part of the new system.

By April of 1933, the USG consisted of fifteen colleges and universities, down from twenty-six (which included two agricultural experiment stations). Three were designated for black students: four-year Georgia State Industrial College (now Savannah State University); two-year Agricultural, Industrial & Normal School (now Albany State University); and two-year State Teachers & Agricultural College (now Fort Valley State

---

[4] Ibid., 5. The members of the committee were George F. Zook, president of the University of Akron; Lotus D. Coffman, president of the University of Minnesota; Charles H. Judd, dean of education at the University of Chicago; Edward C. Elliott, president of Purdue University; and George A. Works, professor of higher education at the University of Chicago. Dr. Works served as chair of the committee.

[5] Fincher, *Historical Development*, 5, 9.

University). And two were designated for white women: four-year GSCW and four-year Georgia State Woman's College (GSWC, now Valdosta State University).[6]

The two four-year institutions for white women in the new system, GSCW and GSWC, were part of a dying breed. In 1932, there were only nine state-supported institutions for women in the whole country, and eight of them were located in the South. Georgia was the only state to have two.[7] Single-sex institutions were becoming coed, although GSWC held out until 1950 and GSCW until 1967. During the first half of the twentieth century the number of women enrolled in college in the United States was small but had steadily increased since 1900. In 1900, only 2.8 percent (85,000) of all women of traditional college age, eighteen to twenty-one, were enrolled in college. By 1950, the number of women college students had increased to 17.9 percent (806,000) of all women aged eighteen to twenty-one.[8] Of the 85,000 women enrolled in 1900, 28.6 percent were attending women's colleges. But as more women entered college, they enrolled in coed institutions. Of the women enrolled in 1950, only 12 percent were enrolled in women's colleges.[9]

In 1932, when GSCW came under the jurisdiction of the new system, its fall enrollment was 1,170 students, slightly less than the fall 1929 enrollment.[10] GSWC in Valdosta enrolled a significantly smaller number of students in the early 1920s. In

---

[6] Ibid., 2.

[7] Hair et al., *A Centennial History*, 161. Hair, who wrote chapter 10, "Into the System," does not mention whether or not these nine state-supported institutions for women were for white women only.

[8] Newcomer, *A Century of Higher Education*, 46, table 2.

[9] Ibid., 49, table 3.

[10] Hair et al., *A Centennial History*, 159.

1922, they enrolled only 402 undergraduates.[11] GSWC and GSCW competed for students, and tough economic times exacerbated that competition. President Wells often urged the board of regents to turn GSWC into a two-year college, although to no avail. GSCW enrollment was growing, despite the reduction of state allocations due to the economic depression—an across-the-board 15 percent cut for all system institutions[12]—and despite there being other viable albeit more expensive options for white women students within sixty miles of Milledgeville: the private institutions of Wesleyan College in Macon and Bessie Tift College in Forsyth.

Enrollment continued to grow during the tenure of President Luther Beeson, President Wells's predecessor, but the creation of the USG meant that business would not go on as usual; locals could no longer make autonomous decisions. In 1932, a dispute erupted. President Beeson; the GSCW registrar, Linton Fowler; and a local banker, treasurer of the college, and a member of the GN&IC Board of Directors, Miller S. Bell, were overseeing the building of a new campus library. The college purchased all the building materials, except for the bricks, from a local building supply business, the Fowler-Flemister Company. When other local businesses complained to the board of regents that they had been ignored as potential contractors, the board investigated. They found no evidence of overcharging, but they concluded that there was a conflict of interest. The regents had approved the collaboration of Beeson, Fowler, and Bell on a "building committee" but apparently were unaware that Beeson and Fowler owned stock in Fowler-Flemister. This conflict of interest, in addition to President Beeson's age and ill

---

[11] "History" page, the website for Valdosta State University, accessed July 25, 2018, https://www.valdosta.edu/about/facts/history.php.

[12] Altman, "Marvin S. Pittman," 61.

health, contributed to his forced resignation. On April 6, 1934, Chancellor Phillip Weltner asked for President Beeson's resignation,[13] and the following year Guy Herbert Wells became president.

Guy Herbert Wells: President of South Georgia Teachers College (1926–1934)

Before coming to GSCW, President Wells served as president of SGTC, which prospered under his leadership. Enrollment increased, the two-year institution became four-year, the teacher education program received state and regional recognition, and President Wells beautified the campus.[14] The YWCA at SGTC was not as active as the YWCA at GSCW but President Wells looked for ways to support it. In his second year as president, in 1927, he invited YWCA National Student Secretary Katherine Butler from the YWCA headquarters in New York City to speak at the college in hopes that she could help revive the campus chapter.[15] It is not clear whether she spoke at the college or not.

One of President Wells's major accomplishments at SGTC was to transform the college from a two-year institution to a four-year institution. In 1929, this made SGTC one of only two four-year, public coed colleges in the state. President Wells worked closely with his friend, mentor, and former member of the Georgia legislature, Howell Cone, to make the transition. Cone was a farmer from a small town near Statesboro, called Ivanhoe. He met President Wells when he drove to the countryside looking for dogwoods and crepe myrtles to plant on

---

[13] Hair et al., *A Centennial History*, 166–67.
[14] Altman, "Marvin S. Pittman," 41.
[15] Presley, discussion.

campus. Cone interpreted President Wells's foray into the countryside as a sign of integrity and personal commitment to the school. After this chance meeting, their friendship grew, and they became productive colleagues.[16] Cone and President Wells remained close friends even after he left Statesboro.

President Wells had an interactional, political skill that Delma Presley believed he learned from Cone. President Wells referred to his political skill as knowing "how to walk through a fodder field without rustling a single blade."[17] He said that this aptitude was of particular use when, as a liberal administrator, he found himself in a political "hot spot" with a conservative. This skill, according to Presley, allowed the president to cultivate professional relationships across political divides. For example, Presley spoke of President Wells's respectful relationship with Robert J. H. DeLoach, a strong supporter of right-wing conservative Eugene Talmadge. DeLoach, said Presley, praised President Wells in conversations with his political acquaintances and suggested to the president and to others that he would make a good chancellor of the USG.

It is safe to assume that President Wells had liberal values before he became president of SGTC. While working on his master's degree from Columbia University, he must have taken courses from William Heard Kilpatrick, who taught at Columbia from 1909 to 1937. Kilpatrick was a native Georgian and well-known liberal educator with progressive views on race and religion. His questioning of his own religious values and his effort to teach students to think critically about their values as well created conflict with local clergy and with board members

---

[16] Presley, discussion Ibid.

[17] President Wells to Howell Cone, March 25, 1938, Office of the President, Guy Herbert Wells, 1937–1938, box 1, folder 2, "Howell Cone," Special Collections, Georgia College.

at Mercer University in Macon, Georgia, a then Baptist-affiliated university. Kilpatrick served as acting president at Mercer from 1904 to 1906. After a long and acrimonious hearing with the trustees, Kilpatrick submitted his resignation. Over time, the relationship improved, and in 1926, Mercer University administrators awarded him an honorary doctorate (an LLD).[18] Even if Kilpatrick did not influence President Wells while he was at Columbia, they eventually were close associates and in the 1940s corresponded regularly during the turbulent politics of the state of Georgia.

Early in his presidency at SGTC, President Wells took action based on his liberal values. He worked closely with the president of Georgia State Industrial College for Colored Youths (now Savannah State), Benjamin F. Hubert. Georgia State Industrial College was an 1890 land-grant institution and one of the three colleges for blacks in the state. It became part of the USG in 1932. President Hubert was born into a landholding black family in Hancock County, Georgia, just east of Milledgeville. Hubert's Springfield community was a self-sustaining neighborhood of African American farmers, educators, and entrepreneurs who worked to persuade young people to commit to life in rural areas. Advocates such as those in Springfield were part of the country life movement of the early twentieth century. President Hubert himself was a strong supporter, and, in 1928, established the Association for the Advancement of Negro Country Life.[19] According to Presley, President Hubert and President Wells worked closely together to bring renowned scientist George Washington Carver to Statesboro. They organized public talks by Carver and accompanied him as they traveled across the state. There were blacks and

---

[18] Lounsbury, "William Heard Kilpatrick," 2, 3.
[19] Schultz, *Beyond Forty Acres*, 85.

whites in the audience, although it is unclear if there was integrated seating.

The Carver speaking events occurred just as Governor Russell was creating the university system. Presley's theory is that once the system was established and decisions began to be made about consolidation and transfers, the board of regents punished President Wells for his collaboration with Hubert and Carver. Presley's thinking was that the board assumed that if they moved President Wells to a small college in a small, isolated rural town such as Milledgeville, he would do less harm to the rule of white supremacy.[20] SGTC was a major center for teacher education and thus a potentially powerful training ground for liberal educators. Presley reasoned that the board of regents would have wanted to avoid such influence on students.

In addition, President Wells's transfer could have been punishment because GSCW was considered less prestigious than SGTC, not only because it enrolled fewer students, but because it was a college for women. Or perhaps the board was sending a message simply by moving him somewhere he did not want to go. Historian William Ivy Hair also wondered why President Wells was transferred to GSCW. He did not theorize that President Wells was punished for his liberal values, but the fact that he wondered at all lends credence to Presley's theory. Hair wrote, "Wells lacked polish. Some of his humorous stories were indelicate and his grammar occasionally left something to be desired. With these surface flaws, it might be wondered why such a man was chosen to head a straitlaced woman's college." But he "would prove himself," observed Hair, "to be a leader of sterling qualities."[21]

---

[20] Presley, discussion.
[21] Hair et al., *A Centennial History*, 171–72.

Regardless of whether or not the board of regents sent President Wells to Milledgeville as punishment, while at GSCW, President Wells learned to play it safe in the middle. He learned that his liberal values on race would have to take a back seat in an antiblack political culture based on Jim Crow segregation. He could not always act on his own liberal values when doing so could jeopardize his position and possibly state appropriations. Guy Wells was already politically astute, as Presley attested, but while at GSCW he became even more skilled at his ability to play the middle.

The Founding and Culture of GN&IC/GSCW?

Georgia Normal & Industrial College was established in 1889, primarily through the efforts of Susan Cobb Milton, the wife of Georgia state legislator William Y. Atkinson, who later became governor. Susan Milton encouraged her husband to introduce a bill that would secure funds for the college, and after a series of setbacks, GN&IC opened its doors for classes in 1891 to eighty-eight students from around the state.[22]

Julia A. Flisch was also instrumental in helping pass legislation to establish GN&IC. She was a novelist, a journalist for the Augusta *Chronicle*, and a popular teacher. At GN&IC, she taught stenography, typewriting, telegraphy, and ancient and medieval history. And she was one of the few teachers at GN&IC who held a master's degree.[23] Flisch argued that since Georgia Institute of Technology (Georgia Tech) and the University of Georgia (UGA) were open to (white) men, it was only fitting that (white) women be trained for teaching, office work, and other jobs associated with what were seen as women's tal-

---

[22] Ibid., 15.
[23] Ibid., 8–9, 14.

26

ents and duties. Students at GN&IC and women students at SGTC were much like the majority of college women across the country in that they were training to be teachers. During the second half of the nineteenth century, more than half of all women in college were attending normal schools and teacher colleges.[24]

South Georgia Teachers College, like GN&IC/GSCW, focused on educating future teachers. At GN&IC, only the last two years were at the college level of instruction; the first two years were more akin to the tenth and eleventh grades of high school.[25] Public schools in the state did not yet offer a twelfth-grade level of education. As such, students at both GSCW and SGTC were very young compared to today's students. At GN&IC/GSCW, a student had to be at least fourteen years old to attend, and the average age was about seventeen.[26]

College for young women during this time was character-ized by strict rules. For example, at SGTC in 1931, there were rules for dating: "Girls are allowed two dates each month, pro-vided the matron has permission from their parents or guardi-ans. The boys may stay only one and one-half hours each time. Sunday night is date night.... Young ladies do not ride to or from town with young men." When the young women and men walked across the main campus, they had to walk on opposite sides of the sidewalk.[27] At a coed college, these rules must have seemed especially unfair to the women, given that men were on the same campus and were much freer to roam about.

In contrast, since all students were women at GSCW, all students' behavior was equally restricted. Dorm "mothers" kept

---

[24] Newcomer, *A Century of Higher Education*, 88.
[25] Hair et al., *A Centennial History*, 17.
[26] Ibid., 53.
[27] Altman, "Marvin S. Pittman," 60.

close watch on the students. They were required to sign in and out of dorms and were generally forbidden to venture off campus alone. These strict rules created an atmosphere of being sheltered, although some alumnae saw it more as a prison. To them, the college retained the feel of the former penitentiary that had been located on what became the grounds of the college from 1817 until the 1870s.[28] Elizabeth Shreve Ryan, a 1946 graduate of GSCW, whose mother attended GN&IC, spoke of students' response to the strict rules during her own time at the college, as well as her mother's: "A lot of these girls greatly resented all of the restrictions. They wouldn't put up with it today. But at that time, that was not anything unusual."[29]

Chapel attendance was required for GN&IC/GSCW students, despite being a public college. Each day began with a Bible reading and a prayer, and up until at least the late 1930s faculty and students were required to attend chapel on four weekday mornings.[30] Students were required to wear their formal uniform at chapel services and their casual uniform for everyday wear.[31] In 1929, seniors had the option to wear the uniform, and in 1934, the requirement was eliminated for all students.[32] In addition to Bible reading and prayer, chapel consisted of nonreligious announcements and programs of general interest. The strict Christian atmosphere attracted parents in the region. Former GN&IC/GSCW presidents J. Harris Chappell (1891–1906) and Marvin McTyeire Parks (1906–1926) were recognized across the state as being "capable educa-

---

[28] Hair et al., *A Centennial History*, 21.

[29] Elizabeth Shreve Ryan (1946 graduate of GSCW), in discussion with author, April 24, 2006, transcript in author's possession.

[30] Hair et al., *A Centennial History*, 176.

[31] Ibid., 42.

[32] Ibid., 125, 175.

tors and Christian gentlemen."[33] The Christian culture of the college fit splendidly with the mission of the YWCA to build "Christian character" among its students. By the mid-1920s, however, the campus YWCA taught that a Christian character should include action against social problems.

Given this strict atmosphere, Georgia College historian Edward Dawson asked why might a young woman choose GN&IC over other (white) women's colleges in Georgia such as Wesleyan in Macon, LaGrange College in LaGrange, Shorter in Rome, or Agnes Scott in Decatur? Dawson speculated that, first of all, parents chose for the students, and, secondly, tuition was cheap. Citing the *GN&IC Bulletin*, he noted that "until 1917, 'The entire cost of a year's attendance' came to 'about $130, not counting books, clothing, railroad fare, and incidental expenses.'"[34] Twenty-six years later, in 1943, the tuition was still relatively low. In 1943, Helen Matthews Lewis transferred to GSCW from Bessie Tift College because her parents could no longer afford the tuition.

Tuition remained low, but once President Wells arrived on campus in July of 1934, the culture of GSCW began to change. He raised academic standards, hired new staff, and relaxed the rules.[35] One of the first changes he made was to establish the position of dean of women. He hired Ethel Adams, who had served as the "dean of girls" at Griffin High School in East Central Georgia. President Wells and Dean Adams worked well together and agreed on ways to improve the college experience for students. One of the most famous and successful new ideas was Dean Adams's introduction of the Golden Slipper ritual that brought students together in competition for the best

---

[33] Hair et al., 88.
[34] Ibid., 88
[35] Ibid., 174.

play. The winning class was given a replica of a women's dressy evening shoe made of pewter with gold plating. It was a strong tradition that created a deep sense of community among students and lasted until the 1970s. President Wells also hired Hoy Taylor as the academic dean, whom he brought along with him from SGTC. President Wells was also responsible for increasing the number of faculty with graduate degrees, from 31.8 percent in 1928–1929 to 93.3 percent in 1938–1939.[36]

Under President Wells, required uniforms and required chapel attendance became rules of the past, and loosening these rules created a space for student voices that had not existed before.[37] The College Government Association began to form during the last year of President Beeson's administration and during President Wells's tenure grew into a viable campus organization. The student newspaper, *The Colonnade*, reflected the new student voice as it was uncensored by faculty or administration. Hair observed, "Unlike most college newspapers of that era, no faculty member or administrator censored, wrote, or even read stories or editorials before they were printed. It was indeed 'a student organ entirely.'"[38] The campus chapter of the YWCA had its own editor on *The Colonnade* staff from 1925 through 1939. Throughout the 1930s and 1940s the YWCA had a strong voice in *The Colonnade*, covering events and critiquing state and federal policies such as the poll tax, United States isolationism, and the racial order itself.

Marguerite Jernigan, president of the campus chapter of the YWCA in 1938–1939, was a frequent contributor to *The*

---

[36] "Appropriations for State-supported Colleges," Office of the President, Guy H. Wells, 1939–1940, A–L, box 2, folder "Appropriations for State-supported Colleges," Special Collections, Georgia College.

[37] Hair et al., *A Centennial History*, 175.

[38] Ibid., 179.

Colonnade. Her 1940 article on the $1 poll tax in Georgia appeared in the award-winning column "It Looks From Here." Jernigan's article exemplified students' ability to speak out on political issues. She explained that the undemocratic poll tax was in effect in eight Southern states and that if a person did not pay the tax at the polls, the debt would accumulate over the years and would have to be paid before one would be eligible to vote.

In addition to the cumulative nature of the tax, Jernigan identified another major problem. "There is open admission in every state," she noted, "that a large number, in some cases a majority of the poll tax receipts, are paid for by politicians who hold them and vote them wholesale."[39] Jernigan referred to how elected officials or employers sometimes paid a voter's poll tax and pressured them to vote a certain way. During this time, how a person voted could be tracked by the numbered ballot system. The poll tax, she argued, "arose not immediately following the Civil War as many people think, but rather it was a result of the white supremacy conventions that came in the late 1890's and earlier 1900's."[40]

Leaders in the GSCW YWCA educated white students like Jernigan about racism and economic oppression, and they, in turn, were inspired to educate others. The YWCA raised the consciousness of many white college women in the South and helped them think beyond the boundaries of the status quo.

---

[39] Margarite [*sic*] Jernigan, "It Looks From Here: Contemporary Georgia Problems Loom Again in Poll Tax," *The Colonnade* (January 20, 1940): 2.

[40] Jernigan, "It Looks From Here," *Colonnade* (January 20, 1940): 2 Ibid.

The YWCA at GN&IC/GSCW

The YWCA at Georgia Normal & Industrial College was founded in 1895, just six years after the college was established. In the early years, the YWCA was one of only two extracurricular organizations. The other organization was the Recreation Association. In the 1930s, the College Government Association emerged as a third extracurricular opportunity for students. Academic clubs also existed, but membership was smaller compared to the three main student organizations.

Math professor Alice Napier was the YWCA's first faculty sponsor[41] with thirty-five charter members.[42] In the first and only "Y.W.C.A. Issue" of *The Colonnade*, published on March 16, 1927, the author described the purpose of the YWCA as threefold. Students sought to be more "Christlike," to "promote growth in Christian character and service through physical, social mental [*sic*] and spiritual development," and to "share in extending real fellowship throughout the world."

For students, the YWCA was the main artery of the flow of campus information. Prior to *The Colonnade*'s first publication in 1925, the YWCA campus publication, *Triangled Thoughts*—referring to the triangle as the YWCA symbol—served as the only student newspaper.[43] The YWCA also published a handbook for all new students from the fall of 1920 to the spring of 1940.

---

[41] Hair et al., *A Centennial History*, 135.

[42] "'Y' Charter Member of National Association," *The Colonnade* 1 (March 16, 1927). The *Spectrum* of 1928 indicates there were thirty-three charter members. Special Collections, Georgia College (hereafter cited as *Spectrum*).

[43] "Colonnade to Reflect Campus Interests," *The Colonnade* (October 8, 1925): 1.

Membership requirements of the campus association were lax, so there were large numbers of students involved, some more actively than others. In 1929, the YWCA membership was "composed of more than ninety per cent of the student body and practically all of the faculty."[44] The only requirement was that students sign a card that served as their agreement to abide by YWCA principles. There was no membership fee, but leaders encouraged students to donate funds.[45] The YWCA fit well at GSCW as it provided students with a multitude of ways to socialize; no sororities existed at GSCW at the time. At a 1928 membership drive, the chair of the membership committee, Polly Sigman, encouraged students to join: "If you would be collegiate you cannot afford to stay outside of this organization. It has prestige on our campus."[46] *The Colonnade* reported that as of 1932, the GSCW chapter was the largest association of any women's school in the state.[47]

The campus association had executive groups from each class but was led by "Cabinet," the highest level. The association was divided into seven departments: social, service, finance, publicity, religious, world fellowship, and membership. Over time the departments changed slightly, depending on what was needed. The association also established committees as needed, the most important one for this study being the race committee.[48]

---

[44] "Do You Know?" *The Colonnade* (January 28, 1929): 3.

[45] The 1920–1921 student handbook, Special Collections, Georgia College.

[46] "Y.W. Has Drive for Members," *The Colonnade* (October 15, 1928): 1, 6.

[47] "Through the Week with the Y.W.C.A.," *The Colonnade* (October 4, 1932): 3.

[48] *Spectrum*, 1928.

As a paid employee of the college, the resident/general secretary (or director) planned and carried out the daily work of the association with the help of the cabinet and other YWCA members. All resident secretaries were considered official YWCA staff and were required to complete training at the YWCA of the USA headquarters at 600 Lexington Avenue in New York City. Moss remarked that "the YWCA did a stunning training job for their staff and brought them into New York."[49] Two requirements for resident secretaries were that they be graduates of the colleges they served and that they live on campus. As time passed, however, the requirement that the secretary be a graduate of the institution she served, at least at GSCW, was eliminated. In our estimation, Oma Goodson (1924 to 1928, featured in chapter 3), Mary "Polly" Moss (1931 to 1936, featured in chapter 3), and Emily Cottingham (1943 to 1947, featured in chapter 5) were the three most outstanding YWCA resident secretaries at GSCW. The National Student YWCA also employed secretaries at both the regional and national levels.

College presidents had final authority in hiring and firing resident secretaries and determining their salary. In 1937, at GSCW the salary range for one academic year plus one summer session was from $1,600 to $1,800.[50] GN&IC/GSCW presidents employed YWCA resident secretaries for thirty years, from 1918 to 1948. GN&IC's second president, Marvin

---

[49] Polly Moss Cuthbertson (Mary "Polly" Moss, GSCW student 1923–1927, GSCW YWCA resident secretary 1931–1936), in discussion with Frances Sanders Taylor (now Frances Taylor Anton), Charlottesville, VA, May 12, 1982, transcript in author's possession.

[50] Office of the President, Guy H. Wells, 1938–1939, A–G, box 2, University Archives, Special Collections, Ina Dillard Russell Library, Georgia College, Milledgeville, GA (hereafter cited as Special Collections, Georgia College).

McTyeire Parks, hired the first YWCA secretary, Blanche Tait, and in 1947, President Wells hired the last secretary who was officially designated as such, Janet Fowler.[51] Records suggest that during these years GSCW was the only college in Georgia with a paid YWCA resident secretary, which could account, at least partially, for their outstanding work and thus high ranking by regional and national leadership.[52] Tait, Fowler, and all the secretaries in between lived on campus in the "Y" apartment located in Beeson Hall. Here the students hosted pancake breakfasts, current affairs discussions, and housed a library of books about race and economics unavailable in the campus library.

The YWCA at GSCW was "very solid," said Polly Moss. Participating in the YWCA, she said, "was more the thing to do than not to do."[53] According to Moss, Oma Goodson, who served as resident secretary while she was a student, worked hard to recruit top-notch faculty who considered it an honor to be asked to participate. Moss mentioned the influence of history professor Amanda Johnson, who received her BA and MA from the University of Minnesota and her PhD from the University of Chicago. Johnson, Moss said, "led me to have a new appraisal of the history of Georgia." Given Johnson's position in the

---

[51] The employed resident secretaries at GSCW were: Blanche Tait (hired 1918), Blossom Thompson (hired 1918), Margaret Shephard (hired 1920), Etta Carithers (hired 1922), Oma Goodson (hired 1924), Annie Moore Daughtry (hired 1928), Mary "Polly" Moss (hired 1931), Mary Elizabeth Dale (hired 1937), Jane Gilmer (hired 1938), Cynthia Mallory (hired 1939), Emily Cottingham (hired 1943), Louise "Bebe" Davis and Janet Fowler (hired 1947), Weylene Edwards (hired 1950 with the title executive secretary of religious activities), and Isabel "Izzie" Rogers (hired in 1949 as chaplain and then as director of religious affairs).

[52] "'Y' Charter Member of National Association," *The Colonnade*, YWCA Issue (March 16, 1927): 4; Wilma Proctor, "Y.W.C.A. of G.S.C.W.," *The Colonnade* (December 6, 1932): 2.

[53] Moss Cuthbertson, discussion.

history department, it is likely that she also influenced Margaret Kansas Smith and Jane Cassels, also history majors. Like Moss, they were outstanding leaders of the campus YWCA and the National Student YWCA during the 1930s.

During President Wells's tenure, the campus chapter of the YWCA sponsored debates and discussions regarding controversial topics such as social equality (racial integration), Communism, and Socialism. They also organized the annual Institute of Human Relations (IHR), which lasted four days, from Thursday to Sunday, and Religious Emphasis Week, to which they invited speakers such as Myles Horton and Howard Kester. Horton and Kester both advised the YWCA and were leaders in "two of the most radical interracial institutions in the South during the 1930s: the Southern Tenant Farmers Union (STFU), which organized sharecroppers [Kester], and the Highlander Folk School, which trained labor and civil rights organizers [Horton]."[54] Unfortunately, coexisting with the progressive activity of the YWCA were racist activities such as a minstrel show. The November 19, 1934, edition of *The Colonnade* described a minstrel show, "Lassie-Black," that was performed in chapel by the senior class.

In addition to hosting debates and discussions on controversial topics and organizing the Institute of Human Relations and Religious Emphasis Week, GSCW students also participated in the YWCA's Students-in-Industry Program, where students lived in apartments in large cities or "industrial centers" with students from racial backgrounds different from their own. Their task was to find their own job and to live and work as "industrial girls" and to learn about labor issues. The Students-in-Industry program was sometimes referred to as the "Industri-

---

[54] Cohen, *When the Old Left Was Young*, 214.

36

al Experiment." At a Sunday evening vesper service, GSCW students were urged to participate in the program so they could understand "what may be done to lessen the hardships of the working woman." Four activities were listed: "to acquaint oneself with actual conditions as they exist today," "to know the laws relating to working women," "to aid in creating public opinion against undesirable conditions," and "to influence law makers."[55] *The Colonnade* described the itinerary: "In 1929 a group of college girls, probably interracial, will meet in Chicago to work for six weeks with their hands, for wages.... Each student finds her own job in the industry of her choice or wherever employment is available. Seminar sessions of the group meet once or twice a week to consider problems observed and to listen to men and women prominent in the labor and employing world."[56]

No doubt, many of these events were reasons YWCA Southern Regional Secretary Katharine Du Pre Lumpkin placed the GSCW chapter on her list of the most promising campus associations. After surveying forty-seven campuses in the Southeast, Lumpkin identified thirteen associations as the most active and showing the most promise; GSCW was one of those associations. Lumpkin noted in her 1925 report that the students were a "fine group" and exhibited a "good spirit."[57] In 1926, Lumpkin's replacement, Elizabeth (Betty) Webb, report-

---

[55] "Women of Industry' Is Emphasis Presented by Y.W.C.A. Leader," *The Colonnade* (April 7, 1926): 1.

[56] "Do You Know?" *The Colonnade* (January 28, 1929): 3.

[57] Katharine Du Pre Lumpkin, "Confidential Notes on Some Colleges of Southern Division," 3 (August 1925), in author's possession. Frances Taylor Anton shared her files with the authors, which she originally acquired from the YWCA national archive in New York City, before it was moved to Smith College Special Collections (hereafter cited as Anton files in author's possession).

ed that GSCW students were "badly isolated but even this and the fact that they wear dreadful uniforms has not cramped their spirit much. It is refreshing to see what a keen, eager group they have there. They are so anxious not to be 'campus-bound' in thinking.... This is one campus where other extra-curricular activities are not about to crowd YW out!" Webb also noted that the state of Virginia "as a whole is further along in student movement development than any other in the South *unless it be Georgia.*"[58]

In 1928, Goodson was probably responsible for the visit of Willa Young, a national secretary and part of the executive committee of the National Student Council of the YWCA. She had visited the GSCW campus previously in 1915, 1916, and 1918. Her most recent visit was part of a tour of ten colleges in the South (four black and six white, two of which were GSCW and Agnes Scott) to study the campuses' capacity for teaching "world-mindedness." [59] *The Colonnade* reported that "Miss Young is especially interested in social and international questions. During the world war she spent a year and a half in France. The year folowing [*sic*] she studied at the London School of Economics, University of London. Next year, she will work for her Doctor's degree at the University of Geneva, where she will make an especial study of the League of Nations."[60] Young's visit to GSCW is more evidence that the national association recognized and highly valued GSCW members' work.

---

[58] Betty Webb, "Report of Fall 1925," Anton files in author's possession. Emphasis added.

[59] "Curriculum Provides Resource for World-mindedness Says Visitor," *The Colonnade* (October 30, 1928): 6. The colleges listed were "Agnes Scott, Converse, Randolph-Macon, West Hampton, William and Mary, G.S.C.W., and four colored schools."

[60] "Curriculum Provides Resource for World-mindedness Says Visitor," *The Colonnade* (October 30, 1928): 6.

The YWCA thrived during the collegiate era in higher education when extracurricular activities and student organizations began to create a peer culture. During the early 1900s, in many campuses across the country, the YWCA (and YMCA) was the lifeblood of the university since it was before the institutionalization of student activities.[61] For the YWCA at GSCW this translated into committees and events that questioned the racial and class status quo, such as the race committee, the IHR, Religious Emphasis Week, and the Students-in-Industry Program. Given the college student population in the United States, however, students who critiqued the status quo were small in number, but the students who made up this number were more likely than not to be members of Christian-related campus groups such as the YWCA and YMCA.[62]

Although the YWCA and the YMCA worked together to provide some of the first spaces where black and white college students across the South could come together to discuss race problems, the YWCA was a step ahead of the YMCA. Howard Kester recognized the YWCA as having a more advanced critique of the racial status quo. Historian Anthony Dunbar labeled Kester a "leading figure in the South's tiny interracial movement" of the 1920s and 1930s. He was a socialist preacher and worked for the YMCA's European Student Relief project and organized an interracial collegiate organization of his own in 1923.[63] He organized interracial student conferences in Virginia that consisted of both YMCA and YWCA students from all-white Lynchburg College, where Kester worked, and all-black Lynchburg Seminary. Students from Randolph Macon Woman's College (all white) also attended. Kester approached

---

[61] Geiger, *The History of American Higher Education*, 365, 370, 420.

[62] Fass, *The Damned and the Beautiful*, 328–29, 334.

[63] Dunbar, *Against the Grain*, 5, 7, 20, 83.

the YWCA to request a location for these integrated conferences. In a 1974 interview, Kester was asked, "You went to the
YWCA instead of the YMCA?" He replied, "Lord have mercy,
yes. You'd never get anything out of the YMCA.... The YWCA
was always way ahead of the YMCA.... [The YWCA] was
more adventurous, and saw the agony through which Negroes
were passing more quickly and deeply than did the 'Y[MCA]'
secretaries."[64] He was a big supporter of the YWCA but also
criticized the national YWCA's official support of segregation.[65]
Kester spoke at many YWCA conferences across the region and
frequently spoke at GSCW.

Charles Houston's 1934 speech corroborates Kester's view
of the YMCA. Houston was a Harvard-educated attorney and
the first African American editor of the *Harvard Law Review*.
At the national YWCA convention in Philadelphia, which
GSCW YWCA president Margaret Kansas Smith attended,[66]
Houston gave a speech titled "An Approach to Better Race Relations." In his speech he gave credit to the National Industrial
Recovery Act and the National Association for the Advancement of Colored People (NAACP), but he criticized the work
of the Urban League and the YMCA, calling the YMCA the
"Young Men's Conservative Association."[67]

---

[64] Howard Kester, July 22, 1974, interview B-0007-1, transcript,
Southern Oral History Program Collection (#4007), Southern Historical
Collection, Louis Round Wilson Special Collections Library, University of
North Carolina at Chapel Hill.

[65] Taylor, "On the Edge of Tomorrow," 154.

[66] "Y Leader Presides at National Council," *The Colonnade* (May 11,
1934): 3.

[67] "An Approach to Better Race Relations" page, the website for Legal
Information Institute of Cornell Law School, accessed June 9, 2016,
https://www.law.cornell.edu/houston/ywcatxt.htm. Thanks to historian Patricia Sullivan for suggesting the author look into Houston's speech.

In the late nineteenth and early twentieth centuries, the YMCA's mission focused on providing services, especially those that would enhance men's physical fitness and develop the "whole man." This shift in mission changed their constituency from men and boys of all classes to predominantly middle-class men and boys. This shift also created a building spree, and those who used the buildings and services were those who could afford to pay for them. Historian Nancy Robertson summarized this period of YMCA growth: "By 1899, the majority of men in the association stressed activities that were tied to buildings, as opposed to community-based work or reform efforts. From 1900 to 1930, YMCAs engaged in a campaign to build more and bigger facilities and a YMCA building became an expected feature of the American urban landscape."[68] These changes in mission—serving a largely white, middle-class clientele—and the local business-sector governance of the YMCA created a conservatizing effect on the organization that the YWCA never experienced.

Augusta Roberts, YWCA Southern regional secretary of the student division, explained that the white-student YMCA tended toward the racial status quo because they were funded through their local communities, as was the city division of the YMCA. As such, many white YMCA members were often against any type of racial reform: "They had families and they put their roots down with the local Rotarians and local ministers.... They had alot [sic] at stake in the locality." Roberts continued, "Oftentimes these men were a part of 'the old boy network'...where vulnerability for nonconformity was often real."[69]

---

[68] Robertson, *Christian Sisterhood*, 103–104.
[69] Taylor, "On the Edge of Tomorrow," 213–14.

A Brief History of the National Student YWCA

In 1906 the YWCA of the United States of America was established with the merger of two organizations. One organization, the International Board of Women's and Young Women's Christian Associations, was committed to serving the needs of young, native-born, single women who moved to urban areas for employment (often referred to as "industrial girls"), and the other organization, the American Committee of the Young Women's Christian Associations, was devoted to developing the Christian character of college students. This merger formed one organization with two divisions: student and city/community.

Prior to the merger, in 1873 white undergraduates at Normal University in Illinois established the first student branch. By the 1890s, there were seven black student associations across the nation with white associations concentrated in the Midwest. In 1886, the student groups, although segregated, formed a national association: the American Committee of Young Women's Christian Associations. At the time of the 1906 merger, black student associations numbered about twelve affiliated groups, out of a total of 469 student associations that had applied for affiliation. In 1913, assisted by the merger, the student YWCA in black colleges had grown from fourteen associations to more than ninety. By 1922, the total number of all YWCA student associations was 767, which was its peak.[70]

The headquarters of the YWCA of the USA were located in New York City and the National Student Council led the student division.[71] The National Student Council was a representative body elected by students at the annual National Student Assembly. The student YWCA answered only to the na-

---

[70] Robertson, *Christian Sisterhood*, 16–17, 21, 34, 227n15.
[71] See Appendix II for the organizational structure.

tional board that funded them.[72] At the first convention after the merger, held in New York City in 1906, leaders agreed that the mission of the YWCA was "'to advance the physical, social, intellectual, moral, and spiritual interests of young women.' YW[CA] women articulated a vision of Christian sisterhood that provided common ground for those women more oriented toward individual salvation with those committed to social salvation."[73] The GSCW YWCA reflected both these orientations. The 1930s and 1940s, the timeframe covered in this book, reflected a focus on social salvation. The shift began with the hiring of Oma Goodson as resident secretary in 1924. Before and after this time frame, students were more focused on individual salvation and developing Christian character.

The focus on social salvation emanated from the Social Gospel movement of the early twentieth century in the United States. Its advocates were mostly Protestants who believed that the primary message of Jesus Christ was to make the world a more just place. Adherents interpreted the Bible as a moral imperative to end social problems, not an evangelical command to "save souls." Social Gospel supporters focused on *application* of the Gospels to address social problems. Reinhold Niebuhr, an advocate of the Social Gospel movement, advised the YWCA and spoke at many gatherings. Niebuhr was a leading contributor to the progressive political and social thought of the day, as were several of his socialist colleagues from New York's Union Theological Seminary such as Harry Ward and Norman Thomas.[74] Thomas ran for United States president as a Socialist in 1928, 1932, 1936, 1940, 1944, and 1948, and YWCA campus

---

[72] Taylor, "On the Edge of Tomorrow," 13, 213.
[73] Robertson, *Christian Sisterhood*, 18.
[74] Dunbar, *Against the Grain*, 14, 39, 40.

leaders across the Southeast frequently invited him as a guest speaker.

Other leaders in the Social Gospel movement also advised the YWCA, including Paul Tillich and Scotty Cowan. In her unpublished dissertation, historian Frances Sanders Taylor explained that the Social Gospel movement of the late nineteenth century "encouraged Christians to apply Christian teachings of brotherhood to daily relationships. Initially, urban and labor conditions attracted the attention of the disciples of the Social Gospel but, over time, race relations appeared on their agenda."[75] This did not mean that all white Social Gospel advocates spoke out against segregation. But many used the principles of the Social Gospel movement to argue for race reform during a time of racial violence and whites' fear of the interaction of blacks and whites as equals. Will Alexander established the well-known Commission on Interracial Cooperation (CIC) in 1919, which was also influenced heavily by the Social Gospel movement. Out of the CIC came the activism of Jesse Daniel Ames, the founder of the Association of Southern Women for the Prevention of Lynching. Historian Jacquelyn Dowd Hall chronicled Ames's contributions to early civil rights activity in her 1979 book, *Revolt Against Chivalry*.

In addition to the Social Gospel movement, John Dewey's ideas served as a backdrop for the work of many campus chapters of the YWCA. For Dewey, to be educated meant that college graduates were to be problem solvers as they brought their studies to bear on their everyday lives within their communities. Experiential learning outside the classroom was the opportunity to integrate theory with practice. He saw the duty of educators to be that of teaching students how to participate in their socie-

---

[75] Taylor, "On the Edge of Tomorrow," 8.

ty in such a way as to address social problems: "To organize education so that natural active tendencies shall be fully enlisted in doing something, while seeing to it that the doing requires observation, the acquisition of information, and the use of a constructive imagination, is what most needs to be done to improve social conditions."[76] For Dewey, this participation was the meaning of democracy.

Katharine Du Pre Lumpkin, an advocate for both the Social Gospel movement and for Dewey's educational philosophy, served as a prominent leader for the Southern region of the student YWCA in the mid-1920s. She observed, "I do not find Christian students today awaking to present day issues thru [*sic*] theoretical presentation of them. They are impressed; they are relatively altruistic in their feelings; and all of that is good; but they are rarely set 'on fire' to bring in a new day."[77] Through the YWCA, Lumpkin used Social Gospel principles and Dewey's philosophy of education to inspire college students to address social problems related to race and social class.

Social Gospel principles and Dewey's ideas merged in the first interracial program of the student YWCA in the South. As president of the YWCA at Brenau College in Gainesville, Georgia, Lumpkin was part of the small, intercollegiate, interracial movement. Hall wrote that "in college in north Georgia during World War I, [Lumpkin] found herself swept up in the interracial student movement led by the YWCA.... Guided toward a leftist literature in sociology and economics by the YWCA's industrial secretaries, she learned to think of the South not as an icon but as a social system and to apply to it a

---

[76] Dewey, *Democracy and Education*, 137.

[77] Katharine Du Pre Lumpkin, "An Account of the Visits Made with Miss Derricotte to Hollins College and North Carolina College for Women," March 1923, Anton files in author's possession.

critique of racism and capitalism that would grow more radical as time wore on."[78] Historian Robert Cohen also identified the YWCA as leading an interracial movement on college campuses. He noted that as a Christian organization, members of the YWCA were allowed to critique the racial status quo in ways that would not otherwise have been tolerated.[79]

In 1919, the National Student YWCA announced its first directive for race reform. Bertha Condé, a white YWCA member in charge of college chapters, asserted, "There is no question in the United States more worth our earnest study and sympathy...than the Negro question." The national board fully supported this effort and "hoped that the student division could encourage young college women to rethink their racial attitudes and take action to combat racism." As a result of the push to address "the race question," the student YWCA integrated its staff. For the Southern region, this meant there would be one black secretary and one white secretary serving simultaneously. The Southern region was the only region with this integrated structure.[80]

The Southern Region of the Student YWCA and the Intercollegiate Interracial Movement

The Southern region (i.e., the Southeast) of the student YWCA was one of nine geographical regions and covered ten states: Alabama, Florida, Georgia, Kentucky, Louisiana, Mississippi, North Carolina, South Carolina, Tennessee, and Virginia. Taylor estimated that roughly three out of every four Southern institutions of higher education during the interwar years

---

[78] Hall, "Open Secrets," 117.
[79] Cohen, *When the Old Left Was Young*, 213.
[80] Taylor, "On the Edge of Tomorrow," 4–5, 13.

(with the exception of men's colleges and Roman Catholic schools) had YWCA chapters.[81] The total number of YWCA student associations in the country in 1934 was 530,[82] and in 1938, the Southern region was the largest region with 156 college associations.[83]

Active black associations in Georgia during the 1920s and 1930s were the associations at Fort Valley N&I, Atlanta University, and Spelman College in Atlanta. Active white associations in Georgia were Agnes Scott College in Decatur; Brenau College in Gainesville; GSCW in Milledgeville; GSWC in Valdosta; Wesleyan College in Macon; and UGA in Athens. These associations were either visited or mentioned by the national and regional student secretaries as active or they were mentioned as having sponsored regional meetings. There were also times when some of these associations were less active or seen by regional leaders as troubled and lacking leadership, although the GSCW chapter was consistently seen by national and regional leadership as a strong association.

Three of the nine regions across the country had large numbers of both black and white students. Two of the three regions had a history of especially terrible race relations: the Southern and the Southwest. The student YWCA thought its interracial program could be the most effective in these two regions. Southern regional secretaries Frances Williams (black)

---

[81] Ibid., 6, 8n7.

[82] "Statistical Information on Student Associations," n.d. YWCA of the U.S.A. records, Record Group 11, MS 324, Sophia Smith Collection of Women's History, Smith College Special Collections, Northampton, MA (hereafter cited as MS 324, Smith College Special Collections). Statistical report does not include data before 1934 or after 1996.

[83] "Minutes of the Southern Division of the National Student Council, Y.W.C.A.," September 30, 1938, to October 2, 1938, box 757, folder 4, MS 324, Smith College Special Collections.

and Lumpkin (white) organized the first implementation of the 1919 directive in the Southeast in 1922.[84] Hall identified the YWCA and the Southeastern Federation of Colored Women's Clubs at the turn of the century as "*the* most important institutional avenues for black women's participation in the interracial movement."[85]

Lumpkin and Williams determined which cities and white colleges would be the most open to integrated gatherings and hammered out details such as seating and the configuration of small-group work. The interracial program included forums on campuses in Nashville and Atlanta. These forums were inspired largely by the closely allied Student Volunteer Movement (SVM), which held a major conference in Indianapolis in 1923, discussed below. The YWCA program also included speaker exchanges where black YWCA leaders spoke at white colleges and vice versa. While Lumpkin and Williams were venturing into uncharted interracial territory, the YWCA and YMCA also held the typical segregated ten-day summer conferences at Blue Ridge Assembly and Kings Mountain.[86]

Segregated Summer Conferences: Blue Ridge Assembly and Kings Mountain

In 1906, the same year that the YWCA of the USA was founded, Willis Duke Weatherford established the Blue Ridge Assembly, a conference center in Black Mountain, North Carolina. It was a gathering place for white college students who were members of their campus YWCAs and YMCAs. Weatherford

---

[84] Taylor, "On the Edge of Tomorrow," 7, 31.
[85] Hall, *Revolt*, 103. Emphasis added.
[86] Taylor, "On the Edge of Tomorrow," 13.

had in mind a place for white students to discuss and address social and economic problems of the South. Weatherford himself had been a member of the YMCA as a college student in Texas and later at Vanderbilt. In the summer of 1912, Blue Ridge Assembly opened its doors. Between 1912 and 1944, approximately 150,000 people participated in events at Blue Ridge Assembly.[87]

Weatherford was a Social Gospel advocate and accepted the segregated conference system, as many white liberals and Social Gospel advocates did. In contrast, Reinhold Niebuhr opposed the segregated summer conferences. He publicly stated his position in the summer of 1930 when he attended both the black conference at Kings Mountain, North Carolina, and the white conference at Blue Ridge. He drove 100 miles from the Kings Mountain conference to the Blue Ridge conference. He said of the trip, "I would enjoy it more if I had not come so directly to it from the other conference and if it did not therefore achieve symbolic significance in my mind." As he drove, Niebuhr wondered how white Christians, who presumably had a "sensitive spirit," could "escape constant depression at the sight of the ubiquitous evidence of the Jim Crowism, except by rigorous isolation from the race which bears the brunt of all these social ostracisms." He called this state of being a "spiritual agony."[88]

Segregated summer conferences for white students were held at Blue Ridge from 1912 to 1952.[89] The summer confer-

---

[87] Dykeman, *Prophet of Plenty*, 41, 93.

[88] Reinhold Niebuhr, "Glimpses of the Southland," *The Christian Century* (July 16, 1930), box 2, reel 134, microdex 6, "Interracial," microfilm 2, MS 324, Smith College Special Collections.

[89] See Appendix III for a list of YWCA-YMCA segregated and integrated summer conferences.

ence for black students was held in Kings Mountain, for the most part, from 1916 to 1939.[90] In 1939, the Kings Mountain conference was moved to Talladega College in Talladega, Alabama, for the expressed purpose of offering integrated conferences. Summer conferences were occasionally held at Talladega prior to 1939, specifically in 1926 and 1927, but these were segregated.[91] In 1939, black students sacrificed their own conference for the sake of integration.

The black students who sacrificed their conference worked with the integrated team of Southern regional secretaries, Mary Jane Willett (white) and Celestine Smith (black). Willett and Smith lobbied to eliminate segregated conferences and offered fourteen integrated conferences between 1936 and 1951. They offered the first integrated summer conference in 1936 at the all-black Shaw University in Raleigh, North Carolina. GSCW students Jane Cassels and Catherine Mallory, mentioned below, also supported Willett's and Smith's effort to eliminate segregated conferences.

The YWCA integrated conferences were occasionally co-sponsored with the YMCA, but even when they were not co-sponsored, men were invited. Black men's presence made the integrated conferences especially threatening to conservative white college presidents and other powerful antiblack leaders because a space was available for black men and white women to come together as equals where they sat next to each other and shared meals together. In 1946, the national YWCA estab-

---

[90] "The Structure and Organization of the National Student YWCA Annual Regional Conferences: Data compiled from material in the Records Center, September 1964," reel 242, microdex 1, "History," microfilm 2, MS 324, Smith College Special Collections.

[91] *Campus Mirror*, student newspaper 3/1 (October 1926) and 4/3 (December 15) 1927), Publications Collection, Spelman College Collections, Atlanta.

lished an "Interracial Charter" that made integration an official purpose of the national association, not just of the student YWCA in the South. However, the ten-day summer conferences continued to be officially segregated, which created a two-tiered system of segregated and integrated summer conferences.

Other Popular Interracial Conferences in the Southern Region (1920s): Student Volunteer Movement and World Court

In addition to the YWCA and YMCA summer conferences at Blue Ridge Assembly and Kings Mountain, there were Student Volunteer Movement (SVM) conferences and World Court conferences. The YWCA worked closely with both the SVM and World Court, and GSCW students were involved in all of these conferences.

Established in the 1880s, the major purpose of the SVM was not race reform; it was to recruit students to foreign-mission work. In contrast, the secular World Court movement came out of the League of Nations proposals—the precursor to the United Nations—and provided college students with an aptitude for understanding international politics. Energized by having recently won the right to vote, the national YWCA became active in the World Court movement.[92] As with the SVM conferences, World Court conferences were not foremost about race relations. But international politics and missionary work often set the stage for discussions about race as students traveled the world and engaged with people from a variety of racial groups. In January of 1926, GSCW hosted a SVM conference.[93]

---

[92] Maida Goodwin (archivist for the YWCA collection at Smith College) email message to author, May 9, 2012.

[93] "Perfecting Plans for Student Volunteer Conference," *The Colonnade* (January 1926): 1.

One of the most important and influential of these conferences was the SVM conference in Indianapolis in December of 1923, where students were inspired to establish YWCA-YMCA interracial councils back home.[94] The interracial team of Southern regional secretaries, Lumpkin and Williams, worked with students as they formed interracial discussion groups as a result of this conference. A report of the conference from "the Nashville group" indicated that "discussion practically never lagged." The report also indicated that most of the students sat together, and "in presenting the program they usually adopted this division of labor: one white student and one Negro student read papers or gave talks presenting the facts and opinions; one white or a Negro student presided; and a white or Negro student led the discussion."[95] A report that appeared in *The Bulletin*, the student newspaper of Atlanta University (now Clark Atlanta University), noted that the convention in Indianapolis "stimulated the interest of students in southern white colleges in the problems of race relations so much that forums have been started in centers where there are both white and colored colleges" in Knoxville, Tennessee; Nashville, Tennessee; Lynchburg, Virginia; and Atlanta, Georgia.[96]

---

[94] *Atlanta University Bulletin*, series 2, February 1925, no. 58, Anton files in author's possession. Anton shared her files with the authors, which she originally acquired from the Trevor Arnett Library, Atlanta University, now the Archives Research Center, Atlanta University Center, Robert W. Woodruff Library.

[95] Report, "Nashville Group," box 2, reel 144, microdex 2, "Student-Southern," microfilm 2, MS324, Smith College Special Collections.

[96] *Atlanta University Bulletin*, series 2, February 1927, no. 67, Anton files in author's possession. Anton shared her files with the authors, which she originally acquired from the Trevor Arnett Library, Atlanta University, now the Archives Research Center, Atlanta University Center, Robert W. Woodruff Library.

The Bulletin report also provided details of a typical meeting of the Atlanta Interracial Student Forum: "The usual program consists of the reading of two papers, one by a white and one by a colored student, after which the discussion of the topic for the day becomes general.... The attendance varies from twenty-five to forty, of which about forty percent are white. The participants come from all the Negro colleges in Atlanta and from Georgia Institute of Technology, Emory University, and Agnes Scott College."[97] Committees within the Atlanta forum also conducted "surveys on hospital facilities, transportation, housing, education and other such questions of our southern life."[98] By the end of the decade, the average attendance was seventy-five, including both students and faculty.[99]

The "Nashville Group" organized the Nashville Interracial Student Forum. After meeting for almost a year, they invited other students to join them to broaden their discussion beyond Nashville-related race problems to "economic and industrial questions of this and other countries" as well as to add "the whole question of peace and Christian attitudes." The final paragraph of the invitation letter warns potential participants that the meetings will follow the protocol of social equality:

> One thing should be understood as a basis for other things:
> this is to be a meeting representative of all college students
> in Nashville, and both Negro and White students will have

---

[97] *Atlanta University Bulletin*, February 1927.

[98] Grace Towns, *The Scroll*, student newspaper of Atlanta University 32/3 (April 1927), Anton files in author's possession. Anton shared her files with the authors, which she originally acquired from the Trevor Arnett Library, Atlanta University, now the Archives Research Center, Atlanta University Center, Robert W. Woodruff Library

[99] Report by Minnie Cureton, 1922–1926, box 2, reel 144, microdex 2, "Student-Southern," microfilm 2, MS324, Smith College Special Collections.

the same privileges in all respects in these meetings. Those students who come should come with this in mind, ready to comply with this understanding in their conduct during the meetings. There will be no special arrangements of seating nor reserved seats for either group.[100]

During the 1920s, as Lumpkin and Williams carried out the 1919 national student YWCA directive, by organizing interracial forums and speaker exchanges, both the YWCA and the YMCA continued to hold joint, segregated, ten-day summer conferences. And occasionally, even segregated conferences caught the attention of white supremacists.

The 1927 Blue Ridge Conference Survey[101]

In 1927, the student YWCA of the Southern region evoked near hysteria when leaders distributed a survey to conference attendees at Blue Ridge Assembly. The survey asked for students' opinions on labor, gender, and racial segregation. GSCW was drawn into the fray by President V. L. Roy of State Normal College in Natchitoches, Louisiana. President Roy wrote to President Beeson (President Wells's predecessor), railing against the YWCA and their efforts to destroy racial barriers. Weatherford was also drawn into the letter exchange. Even though the conference was segregated, merely *asking* white women their opinions on the racial structure of the South was seen as treasonous.

---

[100] Invitation letter, October 11, 1924, 111 Kissam Hall, Vanderbilt University. Signed E. L. Ackley, E. B. Canaday, W. B. Green, Sarah Neblett, W. L. Newman, members of the "Continuation Committee," Nashville Interracial Student Forum, box 2, reel 144, microdex 2, "Student-Southern," microfilm 2, MS324, Smith College Special Collections.

[101] See Appendix IV for survey.

President Roy initiated a letter-writing campaign to draw attention to the interracial work of the student YWCA in both the Southern and Southwestern regions. In a May 4, 1928, letter to President Beeson, President Roy mentioned that he knew more about the case at Hollister, Missouri, and Monte Ne, Arkansas, both in the YWCA's Southwest region. There, he claimed, black and white students ate at the same table; President Roy said he had heard that black and white students sat together at Blue Ridge as well. He sent a letter to several white college presidents in the South to "direct...[their] attention to the gravity of this situation."[102] He described the situation as a "rather definite effort to let the racial bars down at the Y.W.C.A. conferences in the South." He included in his correspondence to President Beeson a copy of a letter from the president of State Teachers College in Hattiesburg (now the University of Southern Mississippi), Joe Cook. President Cook expressed solidarity with President Roy's cause: "We have also been concerned over some sentiments that were brought back from Blue Ridge regarding the race question, and I shall be pleased to back you in your efforts for sane ideas and sane discussions of the race question."[103] President Beeson replied to President Roy that "my understanding is that no negro [sic] delegates are at the Conference. They usually have a negro [sic] woman to speak to the girls on race relations. The servants [who are black] are housed in a separate cottage some distance

---

[102] V. L. Roy to President Beeson, April 27, 1928, Office of the President, J. Luther Beeson, box 7, folder 1, "YWCA of GSCW 1928–1933," Special Collections, Georgia College.

[103] Joe Cook to V. L. Roy, May 12, 1928, Office of the President, J. Luther Beeson, box 7, folder 1, "YWCA of GSCW 1928–1933," Special Collections, Georgia College.

from the students."[104] Beeson concluded the letter with a request that President Roy "go into detail concerning the objectionable features at Blue Ridge."[105]

President Roy said he was distraught by a survey YWCA leaders distributed at the conference:

> The types of questionnaires that have been presented to be filled out by the college girls of the South at the Blue Ridge conferences, particularly the conference of last year [1927], indicate very definitely that the attitude of the managers is a menace to the social bars that have been set up by the white people of the South to protect their race.... If you can obtain copies of the questionnaires that have been circulated among our delegates, you will be fully convinced of the dangerous attitude of the National Council.[106]

The survey covered five topics: economic inequality, racism, religion, gender, and parenting. Nine statements (31.0 percent) explored economic inequality, or "labor," as is indicated in pencil in the margins of the survey; seven statements each (24.1 percent) covered race and religion; five statements (17.5 percent) referenced gender; and two statements (6.9 percent) referenced parenting. The number of statements on each topic suggested that social problems related to labor and religion were the most pressing for the creators of the YWCA survey, with racism being a close second. Below are examples of the more controversial statements and how participants responded.

---

[104] Throughout the correspondence "Negro" is often not capitalized as it should be. Therefore "[sic]" is used when it appears with a lowercase "n."

[105] President Beeson to V. L. Roy, April 30, 1928, Office of the President, J. Luther Beeson, box 7, folder 1, "YWCA of GSCW 1928–1933," Special Collections, Georgia College.

[106] V. L. Roy to President Beeson, May 4, 1928, Office of the President, J. Luther Beeson, box 7, folder 1, "YWCA of GSCW 1928–1933," Special Collections, Georgia College.

(1) "A woman has the same right to a career as a man"; (2) "A labor union is a good thing for a worker"; and (3) "I am willing to move in the same social circles as the Negro." The answers were

(1) Yes: 270 [estimate, difficult to read], No: 7, Uncertain: 7

(2) Yes: 147, No: 19, Uncertain: 118

(3) Yes: 22; No: 238, Uncertain: 39

Students had progressive opinions regarding gender and labor, but the overwhelming majority supported segregation, at 79.6 percent.[107] No doubt GSCW's YWCA president, Mary "Polly" Moss, introduced later in chapter 3, was present at this conference and was one of the roughly 20 percent of respondents who reported they did not support segregation. As a member of the YWCA National Student Council, she likely contributed to the construction of the survey.

The survey results make the responses of President Roy and President Cook all the more remarkable. Not only was the conference segregated, but the overwhelming majority of white students who responded to the survey reported they were unwilling to interact with blacks as friends and acquaintances, sharing "social" space. In other words, most were opposed to integration, yet the presidents saw the survey as a real threat to the white power structure. They believed that black and white students were sharing meals and that the YWCA was allowing interactions that violated both formal and informal rules of segregation.

College presidents' reactions to the 1927 survey illustrated the threat the student YWCA posed to the white power struc-

---

[107] "Blue Ridge: 1927," box 2, reel 144, microdex 2, "Student-Southern," microfilm 2, MS 324, Smith College Special Collections.

ture. In 1927, President Wells was at South Georgia Teachers College, and because the YWCA there was not an active chapter, he probably had no knowledge of the YWCA's race reform agenda. He would soon learn of it, however, when he arrived at GSCW. Resident Secretary Moss and her students would present President Wells with one of the most challenging situations he dealt with during his nineteen years at GSCW. And being under a new state system of governance required President Wells to learn a few lessons.

Chapter 3

Lesson One:
Keep a Close Watch on the
YWCA

Once President Wells was transferred from SGTC to GSCW, where the YWCA had a strong foothold, the stage was set for his first lesson on learning to play the middle. YWCA surveys not withstanding, gatherings of young white women and young black men, wherein they interacted as equals, were seen as especially threatening to the racial order. These events thus received extra scrutiny and censure. One particularly effective strategy for quashing civil rights reform efforts such as these was to label the organization communistic.

There was one event during President Wells's first year at GSCW that caused him the most trouble and that served as the catalyst for developing his skill at playing the middle. It was a YWCA-sponsored trip to Fort Valley N&I. Fort Valley N&I was a coed combination high school and college for black students located about sixty miles southwest of Milledgeville. It was not part of the USG at the time but was later adopted by the system in 1939, when it merged with the USG's State Teachers' and Agricultural College in Forsyth and became Fort Valley State College.[1] Public knowledge about this event and

---

[1] Fincher, *Historical Development*, 5.

similar others sponsored by the YWCA drove President Wells to write letters, sometimes in defense of the women, and sometimes threatening them. Often, how President Wells responded to YWCA race reform activities depended on public knowledge of the event and who served as governor.

In February of 1934, five months before President Wells arrived at GSCW, and about a year before the trip took place, Frank Bone, a white owner of a successful brick-making business in Milledgeville, met with members of the GSCW YWCA's race committee. Bone was a trustee at Fort Valley N&I. At this meeting, Bone "described the Fort Valley Normal Industrial School for negroes [sic], of which he is a trustee, to the race committee....So much interest was manifested that Mr. Bone has kindly consented to try to arrange for the girls in this group to go to Fort Valley sometime soon and see how everything is managed."[2]

The race committee can be traced back to 1928, when it was first mentioned in the yearbook, *The Spectrum*, as an official committee of the YWCA. Resident Secretary Goodson probably established the committee. Goodson was a 1920 graduate of GSCW and served as secretary from 1924 to 1928. After graduating, she taught in the campus practice school for teachers—Peabody Laboratory School—until she became resident secretary.[3] While Goodson was the resident secretary, Moss was a

[2] "Through the Week with the YWCA," *The Colonnade* (February 27, 1934): 3. In the interview with Anton, Moss Cuthbertson explained that a Fort Valley faculty member invited them to meet with Fort Valley students. This author believes it may have been Minnie Cureton.

[3] "G.S.C.W. Far Reaching in Its Influence," *The Colonnade*, Alumnae Edition (November 28, 1928): 9. The Peabody Laboratory School was also called the Model School and was funded by the Peabody Educational Fund. It was designed for student teachers and beginning in 1890–1891, the first year of operation, housed thirty-six children, grades one through four. It

GSCW student and YWCA leader. "She was a remarkable woman," said Moss. "Very bright, very able, and she believed in the YWCA."[4] Regional Secretary Lumpkin also praised Goodson's "splendid work."[5]

From the association's inception in 1895 until 1924, when Goodson was hired, YWCA secretaries at GSCW saw their primary role as developing members' Christian character. But that began to change with Goodson, who placed greater emphasis on addressing social problems such as racism and poverty.

Goodson's Mentee: Mary "Polly" Moss

Oma Goodson was, no doubt, Polly Moss's first social justice mentor. They worked alongside each other in the YWCA for four years, from 1924 to 1928. Moss entered GSCW in 1923 at the age of nineteen and quickly became involved in student organizations. She was most active in the YWCA and was elected president of the first-year council. She sang in the "Y choir,"[6] served on the yearbook staff, was a member of the history club, and served as senior class president and dorm president. In most ways, Moss was a typical college student of the 1920s: white and middle class. She was a product of the new national intercollegiate peer culture and was elected by her senior classmates as "Most Popular." But in the most meaningful way, she was different from the typical 1920s college student characterized in historian Paula Fass's *The Damned and the Beautiful*: carefree,

---

grew to include students beyond grade four and ended operations in the 1970s (Hair et al., *A Centennial History*, 15, 57).

[4] Moss Cuthbertson, discussion.

[5] Katharine Du Pre Lumpkin, "Confidential Notes on Some Colleges of Southern Division," 3, August 1925, Anton files in author's possession.

[6] Moss Cuthbertson, discussion.

conservative, and individualistic. Unlike Fass's students, Moss's college experience transformed her to such an extent that she saw a great need for major social, cultural, and political change. At GSCW, through her participation in the YWCA, Moss developed a keen and unusual ability to critique the racial and class status quo.

In 1927, after graduating with a major in history, Moss[7] taught history at GSCW. In 1931, President Beeson hired her as the resident secretary. She grew to understand her YWCA experience as the basis for her transformation from a supporter of Jim Crow to a strong critic. Moss described her YWCA years at GSCW: "The Y.W.C.A. took a hold of my life. I got really turned around....I was interested in so much of it and the kinds of questions because of things that happened to me in the Y.W.C.A." "As I look back," she continued, "I know that this was what was happening. It wasn't just an activity. It was a part of my total educational experience as a college student. And it built a central motivational structure in my learning process which was magnificent."[8]

Polly Moss was born in 1904 in Columbus, Georgia, into a family of former slaveowners. She grew up around family members who spoke of slavery "with a great sense of warmth." She thus learned to find unobjectionable their orientation to the Civil War and its "Lost Cause." Her grandmother recalled Sherman's soldiers invading her parent's plantation when she was eight years old. She explained that her "upbringing on race" was "very traditional....It wanted to keep what was the concept of inferiority of black people. Any challenging of that social sta-

---

[7] Moss was mistakenly identified as a senior in the 1925 *Spectrum*. She was also sometimes referred to as Mary Eunice Moss. Her married name was Cuthbertson.

[8] Moss Cuthbertson, discussion.

tus or economic status or human status was wrong." She continued, "So I came to Georgia State College for Women with all the brainwashing that a culture could give you on racism, on war, on privilege and those things."[9]

Moss's parents were college graduates. Her father graduated from Georgia Tech in Atlanta and worked in Columbus as an engineer and as a high-level administrator for Georgia Power. Her mother graduated from LaGrange College, a Methodist women's college in LaGrange, Georgia. Her older brother also attended Georgia Tech and became an engineer, and her older sister attended a private finishing school in Georgia. The Great Depression arrived early in the South, and during the 1920s, upper-middle-class families such as Moss's struggled financially. By the time she was college-age, in 1923, her college choices were limited. One of the reasons she chose GSCW was the low cost of tuition.

In the YWCA, Moss said she was encouraged to critique her "education" and her "culture." She attended YWCA state conferences that took her out of her own little "niche." Conference participants, she said, addressed "basic questions about the structures of society"—questions of "race, and the study of the South, questions of peace and war, the whole economic struggle that the South was in....[T]here were many conferences on economic problems" where participants "tried to deal with the farm situation and the labor situation."[10]

Once Moss became resident secretary, history professor Amanda Johnson's and Oma Goodson's influence on her as an undergraduate became clear. Under Moss's leadership, students held discussions on Communism, capitalism, Socialism, race, sharecropping, international politics, and war and peace. In

---

[9] Moss Cuthbertson, discussion Ibid.
[10] Moss Cuthbertson, discussion Ibid.

1933, one announcement of an upcoming YWCA-sponsored debate began, "Are you socialistically or capitalistically inclined?" Also in 1933, the announcement in the weekly YWCA column in *The Colonnade* explained the platform of the Socialist Party in the campaign of Norman Thomas, candidate for United States president: "To transfer the principal industries of the country from private ownership, and autocratic, cruelly inefficient management, to social ownership and control."[11]

More evidence of YWCA members' interest in economic oppression, capitalism, and the power of corporate America was a 1936 announcement in *The Colonnade* that read "Big business has found a new means of putting its wares before the public eye.... The Kraft Cheese-American Canning Company speeches which we heard in chapel last week were fairly enlightening...[and are] a living example of big business's invasion of our colleges for the sake of advertisement.... [S]hall our colleges and universities foster and facilitate such a movement, or try to block it?"[12] The following year another announcement of a campus discussion that focused on big business appeared in *The Colonnade*: "Girls on the Checkerboard will be the topic for the [YWCA-sponsored] World Affairs Committee next Thursday. The factory girl of Japan at the mercy of the forces of capitalism and militaristic nationalism will be considered. Do you ever wonder how our stores can sell so cheaply products stamped 'Made in Japan'? Come and find out something more about it."[13]

YWCA students explored both economic oppression and white supremacy. Moss informed white students that they were

---

[11] "Through the Week with the Y.W.C.A.," *The Colonnade* (February 14, 1933): 3.

[12] "So What?" *The Colonnade* (March 2, 1936): 2.

[13] "Through the Week with the Y," *The Colonnade* (March 6, 1937): 3.

not part of a superior race: "You would hold your hands up in mortified horror if someone were so frank as to tell you that you did not belong to the superior race of the world, wouldn't you? Well, that is just what Polly told Cabinet in the last meeting."[14] A few weeks prior, in *The Colonnade*, an author announced a weekly report on the YWCA's study of race and "race prejudice." This announcement was prefaced with a scolding of the "so-called white race." The author brought to light what many whites assumed, namely, that whites were "the chosen people," adding that whites were bullies because they tried to "show the other colors on the globe just how things should be done." She asked, "Are we beginning to see failure ahead in our self-imposed task? Is it because the yellow, the black, and others are beginning to develop a few ideas of their own that has brought up the greatly discussed question of race, and race-prejudice?"[15] In addition to the more critical and controversial topics and activities, students presented pageants, plays, and skits, sponsored devotionals and teas, and hosted parties (e.g., an unfortunate "hobo" party with a soup line) and charm school programs "for the improvement of personality and natural charm."[16] They also discussed romance and marriage.

Some students saw Moss as one of their most influential teachers even though she was not employed as academic faculty. In 1935, seniors were surveyed and asked to "name five teachers who have meant the most to you. (Name in order, best first)." Out of thirty-six respondents, five students listed Moss in the list of five (13.9 percent). Four out of the five listed her first, as

---

[14] "Through the Week with the Y.W.C.A.," *The Colonnade*, (March 7, 1933): 3.

[15] Ibid., (February 21, 1933): 3.

[16] "Interesting Program to Be Given Each Night in Auditorium," *The Colonnade* (March 7, 1932): 1.

the teacher who meant the most to them. Another survey question asked students, "Has the Y.W.C.A. functioned in your life while at College as well as you think it should?" A strong majority answered yes (63.8 percent). Four out of the five students who commented on their "No" response indicated that the YWCA did not serve them well, but that it was their own fault. One student commented, "It does a few people much good, but doesn't reach all."[17]

National Student Secretary Winnifred Wygal described Moss as "an emancipated Southerner as far as race, theology, and social philosophy are concerned, but she is an intelligent, steady person of sound educational philosophy."[18] Moss was part of an interracial network in the South of highly influential secretaries. Taylor wrote that the "national student secretaries of that era [1930s]—Carrie Meares [white], Mary Jane Willett [white], Betty Smith [white], Sue Bailey [black], and Celestine Smith [black]—and other resident secretaries, including Polly Moss from Georgia State College for Women, formed an invaluable network."[19]

Some members of the YWCA at GSCW quickly taught President Wells that he would have to keep an eye on them. They were young women who were geographically isolated and controlled by strict campus regulations, yet the YWCA helped bring them to a new way of thinking that many powerful whites in Georgia saw as a major threat to the "Southern way of life." For a small group of students at GSCW, as well as for President

---

[17] Student survey, Office of the President, Guy H. Wells, 1934–1935, B–T, box 3, folder "Senior Questionnaire 1935," Special Collections, Georgia College.

[18] Winnifred Wygal, "Report of the Trip of Winnifred Wygal to Milledgeville, Ga., May 12–16, 1935," reel 144, microdex 5, "Reports Misc.," MS324, Smith College Special Collections.

[19] Taylor, "On the Edge of Tomorrow," 73.

Wells, the "wild" trip to Fort Valley was the first step on a journey to a new way of thinking.

The "Wild" Trip to Fort Valley: March 3, 1935[20]

About one year before the YWCA trip to Fort Valley, rumors had been circulating about GSCW and Agnes Scott College. In February of 1934, around the same time that Frank Bone met with the YWCA race committee about visiting Fort Valley N&I, Charles Blasser, assistant editor of the far-right magazine *National Republic*, had been spreading rumors in Augusta at public events about GSCW and Agnes Scott College. He claimed "that there were 'communistic influences' at work" at these two women's colleges and that the YWCA was to blame. The moral panic was set off by an article published in the more popular *Liberty* magazine, titled "Will the Communists Get Our Girls in College?" Mrs. J. E. Andrews, a "prominent Atlanta woman" and president of the Women's National Association for the Preservation of the White Race, heard Blasser's rumor and set about to inform other Georgia newspapers.[21]

Linking Civil Rights and Communism

Many in the 1930s, '40s, and '50s who were opposed to civil rights, such as Mrs. Andrews, linked civil rights and Communism to try and quash dissent. Part of the reason these efforts were successful was that the connection between Com-

---

[20] *The Colonnade* (February 27, 1934) indicated that the date of the planned visit was March 3. Other documents indicated that the trip was taken one week later on March 10, but Mrs. Andrews's letter on March 4, in which she criticized the trip after the fact, is evidence that the trip was taken on March 3.

[21] Hair et al., *A Centennial History*, 198–99.

munism and civil rights (i.e., social equality) was real, in one sense. According to historian Glenda Gilmore, blacks in the South weighed heavily on the minds of Communists in the Union of Soviet Socialist Republics (USSR) and in the United States. Basically, their thinking was that blacks were an untapped resource because they stood to benefit greatly from unionization. And to reach African American workers, Communists instituted a "Negro Policy." Gilmore explained that "a decade after the Bolshevik Revolution, Communists in the USSR and the USA created a Negro Policy that left no action to chance. In the first place, there must be absolute equality between individuals in all social relations.... The system, which most people called *social equality*, offered a simple mandate for all human activity, from whom one should ask to dance to where workers should sit at union meetings."[22] Far-right, antiblack segregationists then created and used anti-Communist fervor against those who supported civil rights, calling them Communists so as to silence them.

Joseph P. Kamp's *Behind the Lace Curtains of the YWCA*[23] is a prime example of how far-right segregationists linked civil rights and Communism. Kamp's paperback booklet was published in 1948, but it featured many events and people who were active in the YWCA in the 1930s and in the interracial movement. Many of his villains visited and/or spoke at GSCW. Kamp was a member of the Constitutional Educational League of New York City that published the booklet. He claimed he

---

[22] Gilmore, *Defying Dixie*, 29.

[23] On the book's cover, the "C" in YWCA is a hammer and sickle. The sickle opens toward the right, to make the symbol appear as a "C." In the actual communist symbol, the sickle opens toward the left. See illustration.

wrote it to document an investigation into the YWCA.[24] Like Mrs. Andrews and many other white supremacists in Georgia, Kamp believed that the YWCA was led by Communists and those sympathetic to Communism.

Kamp mentioned Eugene V. Debs, Howard Kester, and Harry F. Ward and labeled them *"three top-flight Reds."* Kamp also included Reinhold Niebuhr and Southern novelist and social critic Lillian Smith in his list of dangerous subversives. He identified Howard Kester as a member of the "National Committee of the *Friends of the Soviet Union* and a leader at Red *Highlander Folk School"* and mentioned both Myles and Zilphia Horton, with Zilphia Horton coming in squarely for blame for the "Leftist perversion of 'Y' recreational singing" and the Highlander Folk School as "a center, if not the center, for the spreading of Communist doctrine in 13 Southeastern states." Kamp also identified YWCA National Student Secretary Winnifred Wygal as one of fifteen religious authors "who have records of affiliation with Communist or Communist front organizations."[25] Wygal had a long tradition of speaking at GSCW. Kester and Horton also spoke at GSCW at YWCA-related events.

To provide evidence for his claim that the YWCA was a Communist organization, he quoted from a resolution purportedly adopted in December 1941 by the Assembly of Student Christian Associations, which included both the YWCA and the YMCA. The resolution called for "furthering the establishment of a student Christian movement and a social order which provides every individual, regardless of race, creed or national origin, opportunity to participate in and share alike all the relationships of life. *(including marriage?)"*[26]

---

[24] Kamp, *Behind the Lace Curtains,* 5.
[25] Ibid., 20, 27, 33, 37. Emphasis in original.
[26] Ibid., 41–42. Emphasis in original.

Looking back on her experience living in Georgia, Jane Cassels wrote, in an article published in 1957 in *The American Scholar*, that many white Southerners believed in the natural inferiority of blacks and that any effort blacks made toward self-determination must have been organized by whites, and *suspect* whites at that—that is to say, Communists from the North. Cassels concluded that "if such thinking were confined to the lunatic fringe or to cynics who make political capital out of this sort of thing, the matter could be dismissed without comment. But the idea that desegregation and communism are somehow inextricably linked has gained currency with people who are neither paranoic nor callously opportunistic."[27]

The fear of social equality was based in the fear of race mixing that bringing black and white women and men together would result in heterosexual intercourse between them. If it took whipping people up into an anti-Communist frenzy to prevent "race-mixing," then so be it. Social equality was a term that easily brought on moral panic and hysteria among most racist whites. For example, in response to the 1941 race drama in the USG that Governor Talmadge himself caused (discussed in chapter 5), he wrote in his newspaper, *The Statesman*, "I'm not going to put up with social equality. We don't need no [Negroes] and white people taught together."[28] He doesn't specify as to whether or not the people taught together are women or men, but that those women and men would have biracial children together was a background expectation of many such remarks about social equality.

The effectiveness of linking social equality/civil rights with communism rested largely on the control of women's sexuality.

---

[27] Cassels Record, "The Red-Tagging of Negro Protest," 325.

[28] Anderson, *The Wild Man from Sugar Creek*, 197. Talmadge used the N-word.

The fundamental question centered on which group of men should have proprietary rights of access to women. It was understood that men should have access to women as property, but the question was, which group of men. And white supremacist men were clear that it would not be black men. So when the YWCA began sponsoring interracial gatherings that also included men, white supremacists in Georgia took notice.

President Wells and Mrs. J. E. Andrews

While President Wells was settling in to his new position at GSCW, Mrs. Andrews learned of the YWCA students' planned trip to Fort Valley N&I. On the evening of March 1, two days before the trip, Mrs. Andrews telephoned President Wells at home. Ruby Wells, President Wells's wife, answered the call. President Wells was asleep, so she did not wake him, but later relayed Mrs. Andrews's message. She told her husband that Mrs. Andrews said she objected to two student trips: one that had already occurred—a Student Volunteer Movement conference in Atlanta—and one that had not—the Fort Valley visit.[29]

President Wells responded in a letter to Mrs. Andrews that there were times when Christian people must realize that the lines between following the laws of Jim Crow segregation and being a Christian might rightly be blurred. He apologized for missing her call and explained, regarding the SVM conference, that he had heard that "there were some plans for the delegates to perhaps eat and sleep together. I told Miss Moss, our Y.W.C.A. Secretary, that we would object to this." But, he add-

---

[29] President Wells to Mrs. J. E. Andrews, March 2, 1935, Office of the President, Guy H. Wells, 1934–1935, B–T, box 3, folder "Race Situation (Letters from Mrs. Andrews) 1935," Special Collections, Georgia College.

ed, "if the girls were meeting to discuss problems of their future work as missionaries to the foreign fields with people of other races for the purpose of getting information and understanding each other better, I had no objection. I am told that this is all they did....The two girls who attended the meeting...have planned to spend their lives upon the foreign fields." As for the trip to Fort Valley, President Wells said, "As I understand it, there was not to be any social inequality [*sic*] or any contacts that could in any way be interpreted as inappropriate." He concluded, "I believe if you understood the situation and purposes of these two incidents...you could not object in any way."[30] President Wells's response illustrated a leader with political acumen who defended the students by framing their trip in terms of Christian identity. The students were simply trying to be good Christians by learning more about people from racial groups different from their own.

President Wells may have seemed confident in his response, but on the same day he wrote to Mrs. Andrews, he wrote to USG chancellor Philip Weltner, unsure about how to handle the situation. He explained to the chancellor that he had just returned from Atlantic City, where he and three colleagues from GSCW had attended meetings where "the whole program was on how to build a better social order, which goes right down your alley. I thought of you and your philosophy several times."[31] Also in attendance at the conference in Atlantic City

---

[30] President Wells to Mrs. J. E. Andrews, March 2, 1935, Office of the President, Guy H. Wells, 1934–1935, B–T, box 3, folder "Race Situation (Letters from Mrs. Andrews) 1935," Special Collections, Georgia College.

[31] It is possible that this meeting was a meeting of the John Dewey Society. An executive committee met in Atlantic City on Sunday, February 24, 1935. It appears there were meetings the whole week. See *Crusade for Democracy: Progressive Education at the Crossroads* by Daniel Tanner, Revised Edi-

were President Marvin Pittman, who began serving as president at South Georgia Teachers College once President Wells left, Dean Henderson of SGTC, and five SGTC faculty. The president confided in Chancellor Weltner: "Immediately upon my return last night, I had a real problem of how to improve the social order in the face of people who differ with you or wish to maintain the status quo." After he explained Mrs. Andrews's complaints, he said he was not going to cancel the trip because he "thought it most profitable that a committee of the Y.W.C.A. have a right to visit this negro [*sic*] institution with one of the trustees and his wife who live in this town and find out all they can....[T]he plan in no way anticipated a social meal or meeting with the negroes [*sic*] in a way that would be embarrassing." The president added, "I am just as interested as anyone in keeping racial purity, but I do think for self-preservation and for a help to better understanding between the races it would be beneficial for each to know some of the problems of the other. If a college cannot do this, I doubt that we can justify a genuine reason for our existence."[32]

There is no record of a response from Chancellor Weltner, but included in President Wells's correspondence was a 1931 pamphlet from Mrs. Andrews's organization titled "First Message from our President." In the pamphlet, Mrs. Andrews claimed that blacks were trying to take over the South, helped along by the United States government that doled out undeserving financial assistance to them and by colleges and univer-

---

tion, 2015, State University of New York Press, Albany. See chapter 2, "The Formative Meetings."

[32] President Wells to Chancellor Philip Weltner, March 2, 1935, Office of the President, Guy H. Wells, 1934–1935, B–T, box 3, folder "Race Situation (Letters from Mrs. Andrews) 1935," Special Collections, Georgia College.

sities that housed "interracial" efforts such as those organized by the YWCA, the YMCA, and the SVM. Within the colleges and universities, according to Mrs. Andrews, these interracial initiatives taught Socialism and encouraged black men to produce children with white women and to, overall, corrupt young Southern white women in colleges and universities across the South:

> A deliberate effort is being made to corrupt the morals, and lower the standard of all school [*sic*], especially college students, the last with a great degree of success. A much misguided interracial group is helping to take that privilege with your child and mine, while they are away at school. At all these things and conditions we most solemnly protest. We protest at teaching socialism to negro [*sic*] men, if it teaches them that they have the right to intercept young white women on the highway, as was done in Birmingham, Ala., and force them into relations to which death is preferable, but to which they must submit or be slain.

Blacks, then, must be put back in their place. Mrs. Andrews warned:

> We [whites] do not wish to wound others, but we must insist on being permitted to live our lives in that peace and tranquility, assured us by the Constitution of the United States of America. All we need to do is to insist that the negro [*sic*] get back in line, and to be made to understand that there is not going to be any supremacy of the negro [*sic*] race in America. The Jews have not tried to become supreme. The Greeks have not tried such a thing; the Scotch have not made that effort; no other sensible race has thought of such a thing,—only negroes [*sic*] are that foolish.[33]

---

[33] Pamphlet, "First Message from Our President," 1931, Women's National Association for the Preservation of the White Race, Office of the

Along with the pamphlet was an article published on March 1, 1935. The article was probably published in *Georgia Woman's World*, a publication of Mrs. Andrews's organization.[34] The article included a reprint of a letter from the president of Agnes Scott College, James Ross McCain, with the heading "Dr. McCain's Letter Read by Representative Ellis Arnal [*sic*] to Georgia Legislature." (Ellis Arnall would become governor eight years later.) The apparent goal of reprinting McCain's letter and letting readers know it was read in the legislature was to intimidate other white liberals, especially presidents and other college and university administrators. In the article, Mrs. Andrews introduced McCain's letter by saying that it "reveals much, but we can add to the understanding of it by telling those who do not know just what has been going on in Agnes Scott and other colleges, right here in the South, to whose tender care the cream of our young Southern white women has been entrusted." Mrs. Andrews added, "We have urged and warned Dr. McCain that he must protect the girls entrusted to his care; hence his letter."

In President McCain's letter he said he supported "social justice for the negro [*sic*] and to have him given better schools, better vocational opportunities, fairer treatment in economic relations, and ample opportunities for developing a fine social life," but that students were "insist[ing] on parading before the world the social intermingling which most white people feel to be dangerous." He said he had expressed his displeasure to

---

President, Guy H. Wells, 1934–1935, B–T, box 3, folder "Race Situation (Letters from Mrs. Andrews) 1935," Special Collections, Georgia College. In addition to the title, also appearing on the front in all capital letters: "God must be the Father and the White Race the Sire of Civilization."

[34] A copy of the article was included in the folder "Race Situation (Letters from Mrs. Andrews) 1935," but the source of the publication was missing.

YWCA leaders about Agnes Scott students and their involvement in interracial meetings and urged the undisclosed president he addressed the letter to, to "keep in close touch with your student leadership this year, especially along the line of race relations." At the same time, he admitted that "we encourage our girls to attend the inter-racial forum" but the forum, he said "meets in a business way to discuss race problems, but which is not social." For white liberals such as President McCain and President Wells, justice for blacks was to be achieved through injustice; they could meet with whites to discuss justice but they must sit and eat in locations separate from and inferior to those in which whites slept and ate. White liberals such as President McCain and President Wells also distanced themselves from Socialism: President McCain concluded, "For a considerable time, I have been disturbed about the programs for the Annual Retreats held by our Christian Association cabinets. It seems to me that they feature too much the socialistic speakers."[35]

President Wells wanted to fully support the YWCA students. Yet he knew Mrs. Andrews could make matters difficult for him. On one side were Mrs. Andrews and others in Milledgeville and the capitol in Atlanta whom he assumed would support her. On the other side were the YWCA and their race reform efforts that he believed were appropriate activities for white college students. He confided in Chancellor Weltner: "I wish, of course, to be prudent, and I realize that we may have some people here who might try to injure me by trying to mis-interpret my actions.... I do not want to be cowardly and afraid every time a little difficulty arises in the performance

---

[35] "Relief—And What a Price!" by Mrs. J. E. Andrews, March 1, 1935, article presumably from *Georgia Woman's World*, Office of the President, Guy H. Wells, 1934–1935, B–T, box 3, folder "Race Situation (Letters from Mrs. Andrews) 1935," Special Collections, Georgia College.

76

of duty. I shall, of course, be glad to be advised by my chief if he thinks or knows of angles of which I am not informed."[36] As the president expressed to the chancellor, he was unwilling to cancel the trip that he had approved and was convinced of its benefits. Therefore, the trip took place on the designated day.

On the afternoon of Sunday, March 3, 1935, Moss and six GSCW students,[37] Dean Hoy Taylor, and possibly Frank Bone and his wife visited Fort Valley N&I. Moss said that Minnie Cureton, a Fort Valley N&I faculty member whom she met at a YWCA interracial conference, invited her and her students for a visit.[38] Cureton was a 1930 Spelman graduate who earned a master's degree from Columbia University and a PhD from Stanford. She taught in the history department at Fort Valley.[39] Unlike President Wells's account of the events, Moss did not indicate that Frank Bone initiated the trip or that he and his wife accompanied the group. It is certain, however, that Dean Taylor went along, and they drove to Fort Valley in two separate cars. They met in the library with members of both the Fort Valley N&I YWCA and YMCA, had tea, saw a performance by the Glee Club, and then departed. Moss described the gathering of students as "'uneventful' but involving 'a very nice exchange of program.' The white YWCA members re-

---

[36] President Wells to Chancellor Weltner, March 2, 1935, Office of the President, Guy H. Wells, 1934–1935, B–T, box 3, folder "Race Situation (Letters from Mrs. Andrews) 1935," Special Collections, Georgia College.

[37] President Wells to Grace McCurdy, August 3, 1935, Office of the President, Guy H. Wells, 1934–1935, B–T, box 3, folder "Race Situation (Letters from Mrs. Andrews) 1935," Special Collections, Georgia College.

[38] Moss Cuthbertson, discussion.

[39] Taronda Spencer (Spelman College archivist) conversation with author, June 2011.

turned to their campus hopeful that they could reciprocate with a tea of their own."[40]

Mrs. Andrews called President Wells at home two days before the trip, as discussed above, and wrote him one day after the trip. In her letter after the trip, she wrote that he had neglected to care for his students, whom he had "permitted to go from under [his]...sheltering care, into an all night wrangle and intermingling of Negro men and young white students." She asserted that President Wells had allowed the students to be exposed to a white chaperone, presumably Moss, with a "warped mind" and "a small strain of Negro blood." Otherwise, her logic went, Moss would have objected to these interracial meetings. Mrs. Andrews claimed that the YWCA was "Negro controlled...[and] sneaks the Negro influence right into our schools and colleges, bringing pressure to bear to force students to join it at one dollar per member...many of whom are ill able to afford the price of the dollar to pay for their own ruin, and the slow destruction of their own race."[41] At these "negro [sic] meetings," she continued, young and innocent white women come in contact with "the poison of jungle influence [that] hypnotizes them into a state of immorality, and unbelief in a Supreme Power, that degrades and retards their moral and spiritual groth [sic], and of other students when they return from these disgraceful orgies." She concluded that "men of the white race," including the fathers of these women, will not permit their daughters "to be wandering foolishly around the country, meeting young Negro men as well as women, and on just such escapades as was intended on the wild trip to Fort Valley.... Hoping that you may reach a clearer understanding of what education should, and shall be, for our fair young daughters of the white

---

[40] Taylor, "On the Edge of Tomorrow," 137.

[41] There is no record of any required membership fee.

race, and that we may assist you in speedily putting that understanding in to practice in the G.S.C.W. is the most sincere wish of Mrs. J. E. Andrews."[42]

One week later, on March 11, President Wells responded to Mrs. Andrews. She had the facts wrong, he wrote, and reminded her who took the trip to Fort Valley and what they did while there. He added that he refused to allow students to be "kept ignorant of what the negroes [*sic*] are trying to do to help themselves or of what we might do to help them to help themselves" and concluded, "I think it very worthwhile that we get all the facts possible, and that we encourage the negro [*sic*] to stay in his place and improve his place."[43] He paradoxically concluded, as did white liberals of the day, that blacks can achieve justice through injustice; that is, they and whites must remain segregated which meant that white supremacy must rule.

Post-"Wild" Trip Events

The YWCA sent National Student Secretary Winnifred Wygal to the Milledgeville campus from New York City to assess the situation. Wygal reported that "when President Wells went in April [of 1935] to the state legislature for his regular presentation of budget and request for appropriation, he was greeted by a dark and suspicious attack and told that unless he got rid of Miss Moss and stopped making Milledgeville a [Negro] college he could not have a cent of appropriation." Wygal reported that

---

[42] Mrs. J. E. Andrews to President Wells, March 4, 1935, Office of the President, Guy H. Wells, 1934–1935, B–T, box 3, folder "Race Situation (Letters from Mrs. Andrews) 1935," Special Collections, Georgia College.

[43] President Wells to Mrs. J. E. Andrews, March 11, 1935, Office of the President, Guy H. Wells, 1934–1935, B–T, box 3, folder "Race Situation (Letters from Mrs. Andrews) 1935," Special Collections, Georgia College.

the legislature threatened to eliminate state funding for the college and demanded that President Wells fire Moss.[44] Wygal met with fifty GSCW students whom she said "were already so well on the way to open-minded thinking and real religious conviction, that I felt that I had very little to do." She said her interaction with the YWCA students was like "carrying coals to Newcastle." Wygal had a much different experience, however, when she met with some of the faculty. She thought that President Wells had reason to want to play it safe in the middle. "Throughout my stay," she wrote, "it was necessary to be extremely cautious about all my remarks and to be conscious of the fact that there were spies in the faculty watching for ways of 'getting' the Y.W.C.A. and through the Y.W.C.A., the president."[45]

If Moss and the students who visited Fort Valley were aware of the criticism of the trip, they didn't let on; they published two articles in *The Colonnade* lauding the experience they had there. The first article was published in the March 16 issue and was titled "Race Committee Visits School at Ft. Valley." The title appeared in bold capital letters on page three. The author described the trip as "quite pleasurable as well as educational. Many of the students had never had any experience with

---

[44] According to the Georgia Archives, the Georgia Assembly records are sporadic regarding standing committees, of which this budget meeting would be a type. As such, the only evidence we have that the Georgia legislature threatened to eliminate state appropriations for GSCW is this report by Wygal and the 1982 Taylor interview with Moss. The Fort Valley trip is included in *A Centennial History of Georgia College*, but there is no record of the threat of losing state appropriations because of it. Wygal reported that the legislature used the N-word.

[45] Winnifred Wygal, "Report of the Trip of Winnifred Wygal to Milledgeville, Ga., May 12–16, 1935," reel 144, microdex 5, "Reports Misc," MS324, Smith College Special Collections.

cultural institutions for negroes [*sic*]; they were thoroughly impressed and inspired by the progress of the school."

Similarly, in a May 10 article, the author labeled the trip as "research" and an opportunity for students to grow and develop. The author noted that one of the recent "research trips" was a visit to "one of our negro [*sic*] colleges."[46] As if it were an attempt to legitimize the Fort Valley visit, the author linked the research trips to the YWCA's effort to help students "face life courageously and give the best that is in us to the society." Cassels was the YWCA editor for *The Colonnade* at the time, so she likely approved the articles for publication or wrote them herself. It is also highly likely that she went to Fort Valley with the YWCA group.

In June, three months after the trip to Fort Valley, Cassels and Catherine Mallory spoke at the YWCA summer conference for white students at Blue Ridge Assembly to pressure leaders to integrate summer conferences. At the conference, one major topic of discussion was a letter sent to the assembly from Kings Mountain delegates asking for a regional interracial conference under conditions of social equality. Black students made the same request in 1923 and in 1930. In 1930, as a result of black students' request, both black and white students at each of their separate conferences voted not to send delegates to either conference. The delegate system allowed black students at white conferences and vice versa, but only as speakers. In addition, black students who spoke at Blue Ridge had to lodge in nearby segregated hotels or find other accommodations.

At the 1935 conference, black students raised the issue again. They wanted only one conference, and it should be integrated. The only two students who spoke strongly and at length

---

[46] "Y.W.C.A. Benefits All GSC Students," *The Colonnade* (May 10, 1935): 10.

in favor of this effort, out of twenty-three students who were recorded as speaking, were two students from GSCW, Cassels and Mallory. One student from South Carolina had mentioned that her state association was "hesitating to plan an interracial conference." Mallory responded that "we do not gain the consent of our colleges and our communities in very many of the progressive things that we undertake but that we have to go in the face of opposition." Cassels reportedly said "she admitted the value and necessity of working slowly and not causing unnecessary friction, but that she felt that the student group must move ahead in its actions rather than spending so much time in talk and that she did not feel that we could wait for our communities to support us in our interracial endeavor."[47] Taylor described Cassels as "one of the most zealous crusaders for an aggressive strategy."[48] In 1936, during her senior year at GSCW, in addition to serving as president of the campus chapter, Cassels was elected as chair of the student YWCA Southern Regional Council, the governing body for the Southern region, and as vice president of the Georgia YWCA-YMCA. The Southern Regional Council of the YWCA was responsible for much of the radical work of the student YWCA in the South during the 1930s and 1940s, and Cassels was at the helm.

Jane Cassels grew up in Americus, Georgia, and enrolled at GSCW in 1933. Every year, including her first, she served as an officer of the campus YWCA. She served as vice president of the first-year council, president of the YWCA's Sophomore Commission, vice president of the chapter, and then president her senior year. Early on in her GSCW career, she and her col-

---

[47] "Report of discussion at Y.W.C.A. Assembly, Blue Ridge Conference, June 18, 1935," reel 133, microdex 2, "Student Conference-Southern, 1936–1949," microfilm 2, MS324, Smith College Special Collections.

[48] Taylor, "On the Edge of Tomorrow," 122.

league won a YWCA-sponsored debate on whether or not "Education as Offered to the American Youth Stimulates Him to Constructive Citizenship." In a scathing indictment, she and her classmate argued the negative side, claiming that "colleges kill rather than foster interest in politics," "they do not teach the truth in history in many instances," "they educate for war rather than peace; nationalism rather than internationalism," that "American college education has gone into the phase of mass production with the result that more people are being trained for jobs than can be disposed of," that "methods used in teaching are based on stereotyped memory work," and that "unprejudiced race and sex relations are not stressed in the curriculum."[49] In 1935, the same year she and Mallory raised their voices in support of integrated conferences, Cassels won a scholarship to Columbia University to study "social conditions"[50] and was also elected as president of the YWCA National Student Council.

A few months after the trip, life at GSCW on the surface seemed normal, even though President Wells was shaken by the event. The students were probably afraid to respond to the criticism in an official manner, especially since Moss's job as resident secretary and apparently state appropriations were on the line. Come May of 1935, state appropriations continued and Moss still had a job. But the fire Mrs. Andrews started continued to smolder.

---

[49] "Goodson, Cassels Win Debate," *The Colonnade* (April 24, 1934): 1.

[50] "Jean [*sic*] Cassels Wins Scholarship to Columbia Univ.," *The Colonnade* (July 3, 1935): 1.

President Wells Responds to Governor
Eugene Talmadge and the Board of Regents

On May 2, President Wells wrote to the chair of the board of regents, Marion Smith. President Wells explained that Governor Talmadge had asked him to meet with Mrs. Andrews, which he attempted to do, but she was not home. Dean of Women Ethel Adams visited her instead. Mrs. Andrews repeated to Dean Adams much of what she said in her letter to President Wells and "goes even further and demands that we abolish the Y.W.C.A. altogether, claiming that it is a negro [*sic*] controlled and negro [*sic*] dominated organization from the North." President Wells said she also demanded that he "get rid of" Moss. He confided to Smith that Moss "as far as I know has given rather satisfactory service" and that "of course, it is preposterous to think that we would abolish the Y.W.C.A." Dean Adams then invited Mrs. Andrews to Milledgeville so she could see for herself "that there are none of the skeletons around here that she thinks are here." President Wells clarified his position on the matter: "As I see it, the woman must be mentally deranged in some way and would be a very dangerous person to have for advice on how to run a college. I am saying this to you and not to the Governor."[51]

Two days later Smith replied: "I have already said to the Governor what you say and a good deal more. I hope you will not let the matter disturb you and I particularly hope you will not let it influence your course in any way whatever. I will take care of the situation before the Board of Regents if it comes

---

[51] President Wells to Marion Smith, May 2, 1935, Office of the President, Guy H. Wells, 1934–1935, B–T, box 3, folder "Race Situation (Letters from Mrs. Andrews) 1935," Special Collections, Georgia College.

up."[52] It appears that the "wild" trip to Fort Valley never came up at any meeting of the board of regents.

President Wells needed skills to play the middle, as this would help him navigate racial politics and, in the process, possibly save Moss's job and state appropriations. Even if state appropriations were not on the line, President Wells spent a great deal of time responding to and defending the trip. From all accounts, before July 26, when the trip to Fort Valley was made more public, only Mrs. Andrews, the national student YWCA, and members of the USG knew of the trip. And before the trip was made more public, President Wells defended it. In her 1934–1935 annual report, Southern Regional Secretary Mary Jane Willett spoke highly of the chapter and of President Wells. She wrote that student members were "much agitated by incendiary accounts of the Association program sponsored by 'the Negro controlled Y.W.C.A.'" President Wells, Willett said, "ignor[ed] the demand of Mrs. Andrews to get rid of the secretary, and has discussed the whole situation thoroughly with his faculty.... There is an intelligent student group in the Association under the leadership of steady courageous officers. The resident Student Secretary [Moss] is one of our best equipped staff members and the program of the Association is supported and understood by the college president."[53]

---

[52] Marion Smith to President Wells, May 4, 1935, Office of the President, Guy H. Wells, 1934–1935, B–T, box 3, folder "Race Situation (Letters from Mrs. Andrews) 1935," Special Collections, Georgia College.

[53] Mary Jane Willett, "Report of the Southern Region of the National Student Council," 1934–1935, 3–4, reel 144, microdex 4, "Annual Repts.," MS324, Smith College Special Collections.

The "Wild" Trip Becomes More Public

After July 26, however, Mrs. Andrews's criticism reached others outside the USG, and at that point, President Wells's support of the YWCA significantly dwindled. A GSCW alumnus, Grace McCurdy of Stone Mountain, mailed a copy of a charge to the Grand Jury of Rockdale County to President Wells. It was the charge of Superior Court Judge James C. Davis, which was published in the *Stone Mountain News*. In the charge, Judge Davis "condemns a certain school in his circuit [Stone Mountain Judicial Circuit] for encouraging racial equality. He does not call the name of the school; one can easily see that it is Agnes Scott. He then says that the Georgia State College for Women is doing the same thing."[54] President Wells thanked McCurdy for her letter and replied that he was not certain if he would write Judge Davis, but if he did, he promised he would not divulge how he received the information. He mentioned to her the Fort Valley trip and Mrs. Andrews's complaints. He described her as "a zealous guardian of the white race."[55]

On August 3, President Wells asked for help from Superior Court Judge John B. Hutcheson, who was a former member of GSCW's board of directors. He hoped Judge Hutcheson would contact Judge Davis on his behalf and explain the situation. President Wells provided Judge Hutcheson with "the facts about this trip" and added, "If you deem it best you may call or write Judge Davis and correct the impression which he may

---

[54] President Wells to Judge John B. Hutcheson, August 3, 1935, Office of the President, Guy H. Wells, 1934–1935, B–T, box 3, folder "Race Situation (Letters from Mrs. Andrews) 1935," Special Collections, Georgia College.

[55] President Wells to Grace McCurdy, August 3, 1935, Office of the President, Guy H. Wells, 1934–1935, B–T, box 3, folder "Race Situation (Letters from Mrs. Andrews) 1935," Special Collections, Georgia College.

have gotten from some source." Taking a swing at the YWCA and changing his tune from when he defended the students to Mrs. Andrews and others, President Wells said "this is a little embarrassing to an institution that is doing its best and trying to do the exact opposite of encouraging racial equality."[56] There is no record that Judge Hutcheson contacted Judge Davis, but Judge Davis would eventually contact President Wells himself.

Judge Davis was associated with the American Legion and became chair of its "Americanism Committee" in late 1935. The American Legion, in the 1930s, was a far-right conservative organization that excluded all black men from being members; even segregated units were not allowed. The Americanism Committee was a type of precursor to the House Un-American Activities Committee, created in 1938, that was devoted to uncovering "hotbed[s] of Communists."[57] The committee was negatively portrayed in an editorial in *The Colonnade*, on November 18, 1939. The author criticized the committee for being "un-American" for its "outburst" and "drastic action" taken by the group "because some pamphlets on renunciation of war were circulated. It later turned out, to the amusement of all, that the circulars had been printed by the U.S. Government." In 1946, Judge Davis was elected to represent Georgia's fifth congressional district in the United States House of Representatives. He was at that time a former member of the Ku Klux Klan, which meant that he was probably a member of the Klan when he corresponded with President Wells about the students' trip

---

[56] President Wells to Judge John B. Hutcheson, August 3, 1935, Office of the President, Guy H. Wells, 1934–1935, B–T, box 3, folder "Race Situation (Letters from Mrs. Andrews) 1935," Special Collections, Georgia College.

[57] Egerton, *Speak Now*, 100, 328.

to Fort Valley.[58] Many Georgia representatives were members of the Ku Klux Klan, and Davis was no exception.[59]

About two months before Judge Davis wrote to President Wells, his associate in the American Legion, Commander Kenneth R. Murrell, wrote to President Wells on August 8 to allow him to "correct any inaccuracies that might appear" in a report the American Legion planned to distribute at a "Department Convention" in Macon. Murrell wrote,

> The Americanism Committee of Atlanta Post # 1 has gathered certain information which would seem tjat [sic] G.S.C.W. students have encouraged to intermingle with students of negro [sic] colleges. Our information is that your Miss Polly Moss, executive of the Y.W.C.A., has strong leanings toward social equality of the negro [sic] race and that religious groups at the college have been permeated with this idea.

Murrell said he wanted to give President Wells a chance to correct any misunderstandings before the report was published and made available "to the people of Georgia."

Murrell enclosed excerpts from the Americanism Committee's report. The report stated that tax payers would be strongly opposed to teachings of racial equality and trips to Fort Valley N&I, Spelman College, and Atlanta University by a state-supported institution such as GSCW. The report also mentioned the Rosenwald Fund. Julius Rosenwald, an Illinois native and part owner of Sears, Roebuck, and Company, established the organization in 1917 to support the education of poor, rural children, both black and white, in the South. As such, Gover-

---

[58] Brown-Nagin, *Courage to Dissent*, 53.

[59] New Georgia Encyclopedia, "E. D. Rivers," last modified August 28, 2019, https://www.georgiaencyclopedia.org/articles/government-politics/ed-rivers-1895-1967.

nor Eugene Talmadge and other white supremacists and critics of liberal educators frequently targeted the Rosenwald Fund as a destroyer of the "Southern way of life" and referred to the fund as "Jew money for [Negroes]."[60]

From roughly 1936 to 1941, the USG spent $350,000 of Rosenwald money, but there is no record of GSCW having received or spent any Rosenwald funds.[61] Since GSCW did not participate in the Rosenwald Fund, the Americanism Committee report noted, "it is hard for us to understand just why these pretty Georgia girls are carried around and introduced to these negros [sic]." The report mentioned both Moss and Margaret Kansas Smith:

> In Miss Polly Moss...you can see the "tie-in" with dominant national Y.W.C.A. executives as she is said to be pretty thoroughly in sympathy with these visits and racial equality generally. This young lady circulated ["circulated" was penciled in] a questionnaire among the students of G.S.C.W. which, we are informed, was a cross examination of the students to see see [sic] just how far this racial equality idea had progressed. It had been given a fine "send off" by her predecessor, Miss Margaret K. Smith.[62]

Smith was one of only two Southerners who ever served as president of the National Student Council of the YWCA dur-

---

[60] Anderson, *The Wild Man from Sugar Creek*, 197. Talmadge used the N-word.

[61] Bailes, "Eugene Talmadge and the Board of Regents Controversy," 413.

[62] Kenneth R. Murrell to President Wells, August 8, 1935, "Excerpts from the Proposed Report of the Department Americanism Committee to the Department Convention: Sec. III–Findings of fact," Office of the President, Guy H. Wells, 1934–1935, B–T, box 3, folder "Race Situation (Letters from Mrs. Andrews) 1935," Special Collections, Georgia College.

ing this time, and both were from GSCW.[63] The other student was Cassels.

If the survey that Moss and Smith purportedly circulated was like earlier surveys that the YWCA distributed to white students, it asked questions such as:

- Do you feel that there is a natural barrier between you and the Negro? Do you think this is because such a barrier really exists, or because of the attitude of society?

- Do you think the Negro gets justice in our courts, and in our social system in general?

- What in your opinion is the desirable outcome of the interracial problem in our country? Amalgamation of the two races? The two races living side by side on a basis of equality and mutual cooperation, but each race distinct and separate? The Negro kept in an inferior position by artificial distinctions and a close drawing of the color line?[64]

Or it could have included items similar to those appearing on the 1927 Blue Ridge survey discussed asked at the summer Blue Ridge conference for white students in 1927, referenced in the previous chapter. The 1927 survey ignited a heated letter exchange between President V. L. Roy of State Normal College in Natchitoches, Louisiana, and President Beeson.

Not having heard from President Wells, Murrell wrote him again, approximately two weeks later, on August 20. He concluded, "We want to show GSCW every consideration but we are alarmed at the tendencies to widen the intermingling races

---

[63] "Y President Elected National Council Leader in New Jersey," *The Colonnade* (September 30, 1935): 1.

[64] Survey used by a group of black and white students in Nashville who met in 1924–1925 as part of the interracial discussion groups organized by Katharine Du Pre Lumpkin and Frances Williams, box 2, reel 144, microdex 3, MS324, Smith College Special Collections.

that have become prominent in churches and educational institutions. We think the matter can best be handled at a private
conference with no publicity."[65] Murrell invited President Wells
to the offices in Atlanta for a conference and offered to drive to
Milledgeville. There is no record that President Wells wrote to
Murrell, but the August 24 issue of the Macon *Telegraph* included a report on the front page stating that President Wells
"appeared yesterday at the invitation of the Americanism committee to assure members that the G.S.C.W. faculty is not
teaching 'communism, extreme pacifism, racial equality or any
other radical ideas.'" The report also stated that "no other officials of colleges in the state were invited to appear before the
committee."[66] President Wells wrote to Judge Davis in response
to the publication of the report but never mailed it.[67] The un-
mailed letter, dated August 24, the same day the report appeared in the *Telegraph*, revealed his frustration with Murrell
and the Americanism Committee. He finally met with the
committee as Murrell requested then turned his attention to
Moss.

Also in a letter dated August 24, President Wells wrote
Moss and requested that she meet with him to discuss the Fort
Valley trip. President Wells admitted he saw nothing wrong

---

[65] Kenneth R. Murrell to President Wells, August 20, 1935, Office of
the President, Guy H. Wells, 1934–1935, B–T, box 3, folder "Race Situation (Letters from Mrs. Andrews) 1935," Special Collections, Georgia College.

[66] "Legion to Discuss Bonus Demands and National Politics Today,"
"Henson Plan Is Scheduled to Draw Fire," Macon *Telegraph* (August 24,
1935): 1, 3.

[67] President Wells to Judge J. C. Davis, August 24, 1935, Office of the
President, Guy H. Wells, 1934–1935, B–T, box 3, folder "Race Situation
(Letters from Mrs. Andrews) 1935," Special Collections, Georgia College.
Penciled in at the top of the copy appears "not mailed."

with the trip, but it brought negative publicity, he said, and this concerned him more than anything else. He blamed Margaret Kansas Smith for all the race reform work that had been done that had put the college in a negative light: "I have spent a great many days this summer trying to correct mistaken ideas of the activities of our Y.W.C.A. I think Margaret K. Smith started the state to talking about this college.... [P]erhaps nothing would ever have been said had it not been for what Margaret K. Smith started three years before." President Wells concluded, "I think you should know these facts, and I want to discuss them with you in person and ask that a program be formulated this year that will eliminate such activities on the part of the interracial committee."[68]

Margaret Kansas Smith was frequently referenced in complaints about the Fort Valley trip even though she graduated in 1934, one year before the excursion, and, from all accounts, did not take the trip. Given that she had graduated, she served as an easy target. Smith grew up in Atlanta, enrolled at GSCW in 1931, and, like Moss and Cassels, majored in history. She was selected as an outstanding GSCW student her junior and senior years. While Moss was resident secretary, Smith served as president of the YWCA Sophomore Commission and as the campus YWCA president from 1932 to 1934. In 1933 she represented the national YWCA at a peace conference in Geneva, Switzerland.[69]

In 1934, Smith served as president of the YWCA National Student Council. Under her leadership the council deliberated

---

[68] President Wells to Polly Moss, August 24, 1935, Office of the President, Guy H. Wells, 1934–1935, B–T, box 3, folder "Race Situation (Letters from Mrs. Andrews) 1935," Special Collections, Georgia College.

[69] "Through the Week with the Y.W.C.A.," *The Colonnade* (April 1, 1933): 3.

over "the responsibilities of college students, such as the national and international problems, the economic and educational systems, and the question of increasing racial prejudice."[70] Perhaps her crowning achievement was the letter she wrote to her constituents that called for radical change:

> The YWCA is interested in the economic system because: you are worried about getting a job; I am worried about getting a job; and so are the students in Maine and California. My uncle is broke; your father is making half of what he formerly did or is totally unemployed. People are starving in Chicago; people are starving in Atlanta; people are starving everywhere....People all over the country are asking why it is that in days when cotton is being plowed under and milk is being poured into rivers that so much want and suffering is at hand. The answer comes that the hungry and unemployed exist, only because we have not learned to distribute our wealth. Therefore, what kind of questions should we be asking ourselves about this economic system? What is capitalism, socialism, communism, fascism? What are the relative merits of those systems? What causes strikes: What is picketing? What is collective bargaining? What are trade unions? What is the "laissez-faire" policy? What is the relation of religion to economics?... What do we know and do about the very roots and origin of our economic insecurity? How well informed is our cabinet on this subject? What does our campus know? Do we ask "How can I cope with world shaking social evils?" or is this the question typical of us—"Cream or lemon please?"
>
> There is another place at which we found society emotionally tense, economically wasteful and ethically un-Christian. I refer to the mutual hatred between races as a result of ignorance and easy acceptance of the attitudes of predecessors.

---

[70] "Y President Tells of National Conference," *The Colonnade*, January 16, 1934, 1.

But as a matter of fact, what do we know about the I.Q. of the Negro, the Anglo-Saxon or Jew? Do we know Negro or Jewish History—outside of white text book[s]? Have we read Negro poetry? Why does the general run of newspapers print very little or nothing about Negro achievements? Why are we deprived of the priviledge [*sic*] of knowing significant people of different races?[71]

Not only did Smith recognize the problem of racism, she suggested its inherent connection to economic oppression. No doubt her political position came across clearly in her interactions with conservatives on race who scapegoated her and labeled her as a troublemaker.

For all their courage, intelligence, and ability to think critically, as well as their leadership positions at national, regional, and local levels, there is no record that President Wells publicly praised Smith, Moss, or Cassels. Instead, he remarked to the chair of the board of regents, Marion Smith, that as far as he knew, Moss's work with the YWCA was "satisfactory." Playing the middle didn't allow for public compliments of white women working to dismantle race and class oppression, as they would have exposed him as too far to the political left. This was one major cost to students of the president's playing the middle.

President Wells's inability to praise Moss and Cassels is all the more tragic given their accomplishments after leaving GSCW.[72] After graduating from GSCW in 1936 with a degree in history, Cassels served as the YWCA Industrial Secretary in Durham, North Carolina. In 1937, she served on the Blue Ridge Committee for the summer conference, and in 1938, as

---

[71] Margaret K. Smith, "A Letter to You from Margaret K. Smith," "Southern Region News Sheet," January 1934, box 2 reel 144, microdex 3, MS324, Smith College Special Collections.

[72] Author was unable to find any information about Margaret K. Smith, other than that she had obtained a copyright for a song.

group leader for the summer conference. Southern radicals Myles Horton, Howard Kester, and Lucy Randolph Mason were members of the same committee.[73] Cassels worked with the National War Labor Board in Atlanta during World War II,[74] a federal board that resolved labor disputes during wartime, and earned her PhD in economics from the University of California-Berkeley.

Cassels married sociologist Wilson Record, author of *The Negro and the Communist Party*, published in 1951 by University of North Carolina Press. They both taught at Southern Illinois University in Carbondale and wrote a few articles together about race in the South, one titled "Ideological Forces and the Negro Protest" (1965) and another titled "Ethnic Studies and Affirmative Action: Ideological Roots and Implications for the Quality of American Life" (1974). Her writing was extensive, covering both academic and more widely read periodicals such as *The New Yorker*, *Antioch Review*, *American Scholar*, and *American Quarterly*. Her academic work on race and labor problems appeared in prominent economics and sociology journals such as *American Economic Review* (1944), *American Journal of Sociology* (1957), and *Social Problems* (1976). In June of 1973, she traveled to China in "the first delegation of American professional women." She and her husband cowrote an article about those experiences titled "Totalist and Pluralist Views of Women's Liberation: Some Reflections on the Chinese and American Settings" (1976). In 1968 she received a Guggenheim Me-

---

[73] "Program of Annual Southern Student Christian Conference" held at Blue Ridge, North Carolina, June 9, 1938 through June, 18 1938, Howard A. Kester Papers #3834, Series 1, July to August 1948, folder 119, Southern Historical Collection, Louis Round Wilson Special Collections Library, University of North Carolina at Chapel Hill.

[74] Record, "Desegregation Near the Bottom of the Ladder," 23.

morial Scholarship in sociology. Jane Cassels Record died in Lake Oswego, Oregon, in February 1981 at the age of sixty-five.[75]

President Wells's emerging strategy, post-Fort Valley trip, was to play a bit on the left, play a bit on the right, to be seen overall as a moderate president. He tried to satisfy people at opposite ends of the political spectrum. On one end were the USG administrators, which included Governor Talmadge and the chair of the board of regents, Marion Smith (although these two were not always allies; Talmadge appointed Smith to the board, but Smith supported Roosevelt's New Deal, which by this time Talmadge did not). On the other end were the young women of the YWCA working for race reform, individuals who were more akin to his own values than those in or associated with the capitol in Atlanta. Yet he used them as cautionary tales, describing them as corrupted and led to extremes by the YWCA. "I have had a number of people, as they were troubled and told me something had to be done," President Wells told Viola James, president of the College Government Association, "bring up the names of Margaret K. Smith and a Miss Parker[76]...and say to me 'Just look what G.S.C.W. has done to them.'"[77]

---

[75] The website for Ancestry Library, "Social Security Death Index" page, accessed June 13, 2011.

[76] "Students Make Trip to Atlanta on Scream-line Bus," *The Colonnade* (April 22, 1935): 4. "Miss Parker" may refer to Jean Parker. She was listed as one of the thirty-two students who accompanied Moss to the left-leaning Institute on Religion and Economics in Atlanta on April 12, 1935. The list of students who attended the institute included several students who show up in other places who we know questioned the racial order through their participation in the campus YWCA while Moss was the resident secretary. The complete list in the order it appears in *The Colonnade* is: Marjorie Lanier, Jean Parker, Sara Ruth Almand, Caroline Ridley, Ruth Vinson, Jane Cassels, Myra Jenkins, Mary Dan Ingram, Georgellen Walker, Louise

Now that YWCA events such as the trip to Fort Valley had become more public and President Wells felt pressure from the American Legion and local judges, as well as Governor Talmadge, he applied pressure to the president of the student body, Viola James, hoping she would help him end the YWCA's race reform work. In addition to using Smith as a cautionary tale in his letter to James, he asked her for "ideas that you think will help me in administering the affairs of our College." He thanked her and two other students for previously speaking with him about "ways of handling this embarrassing situation [the trip to Fort Valley] that has developed over the negro [*sic*] question." He emphasized that as president of the student body, "You can do more to help the school than any other person." Piling on the pressure, he said that he and Dean Adams

> shall have to depend on you to solve many difficult problems that will arise. We are starting [the semester] with *one problem that is more serious than any I have ever had to contend with in my whole experience.* In fact, there is no problem so difficult to handle as the race question, and it takes exceedingly level headed people to keep from stirring up trouble and doing far more harm than good. Oftentimes bloodshed results from mistakes made by conscientious people.

Donehoo, Wilhemena Mallette, Evelyn Green, Margaret Garbutt, Joan Butler, Virginia Goree, Martha Cole Hillhouse, Doris Adamson, Dorothy Meadows, Viola James, Weldon Seals, Mary Winship, Margaret Edwards, Charlotte Edwards, Nellie Day Thompson, Jackie Walker, Mary Wiley, Eugenia Upshaw, Margaret Pace, Mary Harrellson, Annie Lee Gasque, Tommie Cook, Elizabeth Hulsey, Marion Baughn (probably Baugh instead of Baughn since the Baugh family are long-time residents of Milledgeville).

[77] President Wells to Vi (Viola) James, August 28, 1935, Office of the President, Guy H. Wells, 1934–1935, B–T, box 3, folder "Race Situation (Letters from Mrs. Andrews) 1935," Special Collections, Georgia College.

As a solution, he proposed that the campus YWCA should "cease to emphasize as the main part of the Y.W.C.A. program the race question." He added, "If we can stop attending these interracial meetings, the public will regain faith in our Y.W.C.A. and in the College. We can then go on with our normal life and not be worried that our people do not trust the school." He expressed a desire to promote "liberty of conscience and thought," and that he did "not wish to try to *force* any girl to change her opinions." But at the same time he warned, "Our college must be extremely cautious about activities that are as inflammatory to the public as the race question is when it involves social equality."[78] There is no record of a response from James.

Given the pressure he applied, President Wells seemed to be trying to convince James to do what he had already promised Judge Davis and the Americanism Committee she would do. Judge Davis was chair of the committee and wrote to the president and thanked him for attending the committee meeting and for his "statement to us and for your cooperation with respect to the matters which we discussed with you at that Committee meeting." Judge Davis praised GSCW: "It has given me pleasure to make the statement at all times and places that the situation at GSCW is such that no one need fear that their daughters will come in contact with any influences which could be objected to." Judge Davis encouraged President Wells to tune in to a radio broadcast of a speech by Admiral William H. Standley. He explained that the admiral had given a speech in New Jersey wherein he had stated "that the Y.W.C.A and the Y.M.C.A. were two of the most active agencies in America today spreading Communism." Judge Davis thought that the

---

[78] Ibid. Emphasis in original.

president "would find his address to be interesting."[79] President
Wells replied: "I appreciate your very kind letter of October 11
relative to certain criticisms of the college. It is a very difficult
job to know what is right and a still more difficult one to do
what is right in this day of all kinds of 'isms.' Our faculty, I am
sure, are honest and sincere and most of the members want to
do what is best for the girls for the future of our state and nation." He added that he had discussed these matters with all
faculty and "asked for their cooperation in a sane program that
will keep the confidence of the people of the state."[80] President
Wells struggled to know exactly how to handle the strong public criticism he received for the YWCA students' trip to Fort
Valley and similar interracial gatherings. He seemed to have
been able to assuage Judge Davis's fears, and it is certain that
this required skill to play the middle. There was a cost for the
students, though, in at least two ways: first, he saw them as cautionary tales, and second, their behavior would be restricted.

Judge Davis agreed with President Wells that it was difficult to know what to do and how to act on that knowledge "in
this day of all kinds of Isms." Judge Davis said, "We are running
into strange doctrines in the most unexpected places—so much
so, that it seems that it is dangerous to take anything for granted merely because of the source from which it comes." Using
President Wells's fear of more public outcry in response to the
YWCA trip, Judge Davis got what he wanted and identified the

---

[79] Superior Court Judge James C. Davis to President Wells, October
11, 1935, Office of the President, Guy H. Wells, 1934–1935, B–T, box 3,
folder "Race Situation (Letters from Mrs. Andrews) 1935," Special Collections, Georgia College.

[80] President Wells to Superior Court Judge James C. Davis, October
21, 1935, Office of the President, Guy H. Wells, 1934–1935, B–T, box 3,
folder "Race Situation (Letters from Mrs. Andrews) 1935," Special Collections, Georgia College.

president's submission to his power as the president's "spirit of cooperation." On behalf of the Americanism Committee, he concluded, "I want to again assure you that we deeply appreciate your spirit of cooperation."[81] Shifting Judge Davis's attention away from the YWCA at GSCW may have required President Wells's promise that he would do his best to contain and control the students' critique of the social order and their actions taken on behalf of race reform. Perhaps it required a promise that he would fire Polly Moss.

Moss Resigns

For about seven months out of the year, from March through October, President Wells wrote letters about the trip to Fort Valley. In letters to student leaders, to judges, to the board of regents, the chancellor, and others, he both defended the YWCA students who took the trip and criticized them. He defended them (to Mrs. Andrews, Chancellor Weltner, Chair Smith, and alumni Grace McCurdy) before the July 26 publication of the American Legion's reprimand of GSCW in the *Stone Mountain News* and the Macon *Telegraph*, and criticized them (to Judge Hutcheson, Judge Davis, and Viola James) afterwards, taking sides against them. Over the months, possibly due to the public nature of the criticism, pressure began to build for Moss to resign. Although there is no record of student protests in the student newspaper, according to Moss, students rallied to her defense. She recalled the details of her forced resignation:

---

[81] Superior Court Judge James C. Davis to President Wells, October 31, 1935, Office of the President, Guy H. Wells, 1934–1935, B–T, box 3, folder "Race Situation (Letters from Mrs. Andrews) 1935," Special Collections, Georgia College.

Students rose up in revolt. That was the thing that the Georgia State College [for Women] had to explain. The students would not accept that I should be dismissed, and so they had all kinds of discussion and all kinds of—with the administration and—it became a very tense thing, and so the hearing with the advisory board and with the president and then the faculty committee, and that he appointed, in addition to the advisory board, he said that he'd have to ask for my resignation.... I felt that it would do no good for me to try to stay, so I freed the board and the president by saying I would leave. And students didn't like it...and we had...lots of things happen after that in trying to quiet the rumors and to go on with business as usual, and not spending all of our time trying to save *my* job, but I said the important thing is to save the YWCA...and that *that* was the thing that they should work for, not to save my job.[82]

Margaret Forsyth, national YWCA leader, visited the college to investigate. She arrived in Milledgeville on February 27, 1936, almost a year after the Fort Valley trip. Forsyth was the second leader from the national office to visit GSCW to find out more about the case. Winnifred Wygal had visited in May, right after the trip in March, as discussed above. During Forsyth's five-day visit, she met with the faculty advisory board, the student YWCA cabinet, and the entire student body: "I was quite scared by the numerous possibilities of making a blunder, for the situation seemed tense and uneasy, and the meetings felt stiff as could be. Polly Moss, Jane [Cassels] and a few other students and Board members there have all my admiration for their attitude and methods of work in an impossibly difficult situation. Polly Moss is especially fine."[83] Forsyth's report suggested

---

[82] Moss Cuthbertson, discussion.

[83] Margaret Forsyth, report of February 27, 1936, to March 3,1936, visit to GSCW, reel 144, microdex 2, MS324, Smith College Special Collections.

that student protests most likely did take place, even if *The Colonnade* did not cover them.

Recall that in Mary Jane Willett's 1934–1935 annual report, she expressed her admiration for President Wells's resolve to defend YWCA students and to stand firm in the face of Mrs. Andrews's demand to fire Moss. By 1936, however, the tables had turned and President Wells's support for Moss dissipated. Willett reported, "General situation more critical as Georgia political scene more intense. Regional secretary recommended change of resident secretary to break the personality focus of the situation both for the community and the students. This is a natural psychological reaction in the situation and everything has been done by the secretary herself who has handled the situation superbly to keep it from happening."[84]

Moss explained that the Georgia legislature gave President Wells a choice at the budget meeting after the Fort Valley trip: Moss or his own job and state appropriations. "They were going to get rid of Dr. Wells unless he got rid of me," she explained, "and they were cutting off appropriations from the state. So we struggled with that and it finally meant that I had to resign."[85] Moss mentioned both Smith and Cassels as two of her strongest supporters. In June of 1936, fifteen months after the "wild" trip, President Wells forced Moss to resign from her position as resident secretary.

After leaving GSCW, Moss took a position as the YWCA resident secretary at Ohio State University. While there she met her future husband, Ken Cuthbertson, who worked for the Quaker-based organization the American Friends Service

[84] Mary Jane Willett, Annual Report of the Southern Region, 1935–1936, reel 144, microdex 4, "Annual Repts.," MS324, Smith College Special Collections.

[85] Moss Cuthbertson, discussion.

Committee. She also attended Union Theological Seminary to study with Reinhold Niebuhr, and in 1938 earned a master of arts degree. She and Cuthbertson married in 1939. As a rather prominent figure in modern feminism, Susan Lynn featured Polly Moss Cuthbertson in her 1992 book, *Progressive Women in Conservative Times*. She worked for the Middle Atlantic region of the YWCA from 1942 to 1947 and became its executive director in 1948. She also directed programs for the American Friends Service Committee; she organized volunteers in mental hospitals during the 1950s, and in the early 1960s directed the college student program.[86] Moss was employed by the YWCA up until at least 1961, when she served on the bylaws committee of the National Student Council.[87]

President Wells eventually succumbed to all the criticism of the trip, despite supporting it in the beginning. Public knowledge of the trip in a volatile racial climate with an overtly antiblack governor took its toll. In retrospect, President Wells spoke of Moss's resignation in a letter to State Senator Susie T. Moore. In the fall of 1941, Moore wrote him about a rumor she heard at a Rotary meeting, namely, that GSCW had been "entertaining negroes [*sic*]." President Wells responded that this surprised him since the college has "never entertained such groups at meals or in any social way." He admitted that trouble had been afoot four or five years ago—"problems of racial discussion." He explained, "We had to let our Y Secretary go because of too liberal views on race and questions of patriotism." However, he assured the senator that "this college is cooperat-

[86] Lynn, *Progressive Women*, 30, 32.
[87] "Workbook," 1961, box 750, folder 16, MS324, Smith College Special Collections.

ing in every way to keep the education and the culture of the negroes [*sic*] and the whites entirely separate."[88]

---

[88] President Wells to Susie T. Moore, September 20, 1941, Office of the President, Guy H. Wells, 1942–1943, box 2, folder "Board of Regents– September 1941," Special Collections, Georgia College.

Front gate of campus showing lighted GSCW sign,
The Colonnade, May 10, 1935.

Courtesy Ina Dillard Russell Library, Georgia College

MARY MOSS, *Most Popular*

Mary "Polly" Moss, "Most Popular," *The Spectrum*, 1927. Moss graduated with a degree in history in 1927 and served as YWCA campus association president her senior year. She also served during this time on the YWCA National Student Council. President Beeson hired Moss in 1931 as full-time YWCA resident secretary. She served until 1936.

Courtesy Ina Dillard Russell Library, Georgia College

Guy Herbert Wells,
GSCW president (1934–1953), *The Spectrum*, 1938.

Eugene Talmadge, Georgia governor (1933–1937, 1941–1943, reelected in 1946 but died before taking office), GSCW commencement speaker, *The Colonnade*, May 29, 1934.

Courtesy Ina Dillard Russell Library, Georgia College

Margaret Kansas Smith, *The Spectrum*, 1933. Smith graduated with a degree in history in 1934. She served as YWCA campus association president from 1932 to 1934 and as president of the YWCA National Student Council in 1934. In 1933 she represented the national YWCA at a peace conference in Geneva, Switzerland.

Courtesy Ina Dillard Russell Library, Georgia College

Jane Cassels, *The Colonnade*, March 16, 1935. Cassels graduated with a degree in history in 1936. She served as YWCA campus association president in 1936 and as president of the YWCA National Student Council in 1935. She went on to earn a PhD in economics from the University of California-Berkeley.

Courtesy Ina Dillard Russell Library, Georgia College

January 23, 1939

Dr. Guy H. Wells
President Rotary Club
Milledgeville, Georgia

Dear Dr. Wells:

The Y.W.C.A. is sponsoring its third annual Institute of Human Relations
January 26-29. The theme for this year is Southern Problems, having
grown out of the report to the President on the economic conditions in
the south.

The program is as follows:-

Thursday 10:30	Perspective for Southern Problems	Dr. C.M. Destler
	Auditorium	
Thursday 4:00, 8:00	Labor Problems in the South	Mr. Myles Horton
	Ennis Recreation Hall	
Friday 10:30	Introduction to Farm Tenancy	Dr. H.C. Nixon
	Auditorium	
Friday 4:00, 8:00	Farm Tenancy	Dr. H.C.Nixon
	Ennis Recreation Hall	
Saturday 12:00, 2:00	International Scene and its Effect on the South	Rev.Chas. Hamilton
	Auditorium	
Sunday 10:00, 6:45	The Church and its Relation to the South	Dr. W. A. Smart
	Auditorium	

We feel that this program is of vital interest to you as well as to us,
and we extend to all of you a cordial invitation to be present at and
participate in all our meetings.

Sincerely yours,

Marguerite Jernigan
President YWCA

Cynthia Mallory
General Secretary, YWCA

Letter dated January 23, 1939, from GSCW YWCA president Marguerite
Jernigan and GSCW YWCA resident secretary Cynthia Mallory to
President Wells introducing the 1939 program for the Institute of Human
Relations. The program was based on problems discussed at the November
1938 inaugural meeting of the Southern Conference for Human Welfare in
Birmingham, Alabama. GSCW attendees were President Wells, Marguerite
Jernigan, and Mack Swearingen, recently hired as professor of history.

Courtesy Ina Dillard Russell Library, Georgia College

Third Annual
Institute of Human Relations

THEME
SOUTHERN PROBLEMS

Georgia State College
FOR WOMEN

Milledgeville, Ga.

January 26-29, 1939

DR. HOY TAYLOR

Dean of the Institute

LEADERS

Dr. C. M. Destler

Mr. Myles Horton   Rev. Charles Hamilton

Dr. H. C. Nixon   Dr. W. A. Smart

Under Sponsorship

of

Y. W. C. A.

Page 1 of the 1939 Institute of Human Relations Program.

Courtesy Ina Dillard Russell Library, Georgia College

DR. C. M. DESTLER
Historian and Professor
Ga. State Teacher's College

Thursday, January 26

Opening Address

Perspective for Southern Problems .... Dr. Destler
Richard B. Russell Auditorium .... 10:30 A. M.

Bread and Roses for Workers .... Mr. Horton
Ennis Recreation Hall .... 4:00 P. M.
Democracy for Workers .... Mr. Horton
Ennis Recreation Hall .... 8:00 P. M.

Mr. MYLES HORTON
Educational Director
Highlander Folk School

Page 2 of the 1939 Institute of Human Relations Program.

Courtesy Ina Dillard Russell Library, Georgia College

Friday, January 27

Introduction to Farm
Tenancy
Russell Auditorium—10:30 A. M.

Who Are Tenants Now?
Ennis Rec. Hall—4:00 P. M.

The Problems of Possum-Trot
Ennis Rec Hall—8:00 P. M.

DR. H. C. NIXON
Executive of Southern
Conference on Human Welfare

Saturday, January 28

The World Began With Mussolini
Russell Auditorium—10:30 A. M.

The Sky is Red
Russell Auditorium—2:00 P. M.

REV. CHARLES HAMILTON
Minister and Teacher
Okolona Junior
College

Page 3 of the 1939 Institute of Human Relations Program.

Courtesy Ina Dillard Russell Library, Georgia College

Helen Victoria Matthews, *The Spectrum*, 1946.
Courtesy Ina Dillard Russell Library, Georgia College

Emily Cottingham, *The Spectrum*, 1944.
Cottingham served as YWCA resident secretary from 1943 to 1947.
Courtesy Ina Dillard Russell Library, Georgia College

Helen Victoria Matthews, front row, second from right, *The Colonnade*, June 5, 1946. The original caption read: "These politically alert GSCW girls are for Carmichael and don't care who knows it! These banners were held high during the rallies held in Macon and Athens. Carmichael, shown in the foreground, is confident of most of the student vote of the state."

Courtesy Ina Dillard Russell Library, Georgia College

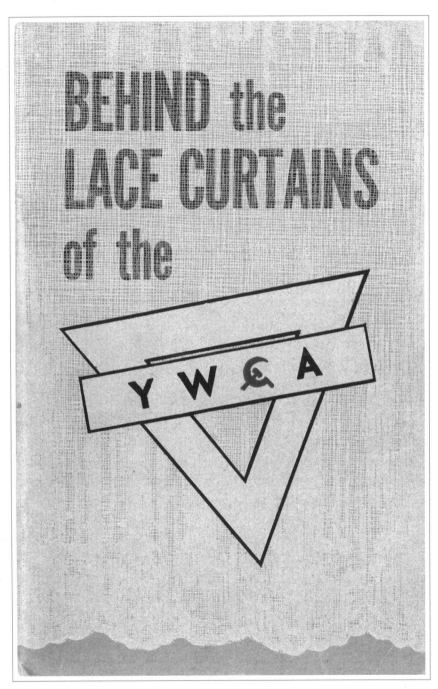

Cover of a paperback booklet by Joseph Kamp published in 1948.

Courtesy Sandra Godwin

Emily Cottingham Stuart and Helen Matthews Lewis, 2010,
Blacksburg, Virginia. Emily's husband, Bob Stuart, in background.

Courtesy Sandra Godwin

Chapter 4

Lesson Two:
Provide Uneven Support of the YWCA

After Polly Moss's forced resignation in 1936 and throughout the remainder of the decade, President Wells solidified his middle position and provided uneven support for the campus YWCA. He began his tenure at GSCW no doubt assuming he could provide consistent, open, and strong support of the YWCA. He had not experienced any trouble with the YWCA at SGTC. He quickly learned at GSCW, however, that showing sustained, strong support would be difficult.

From 1936 to 1939, President Wells vacillated between supporting the YWCA and undermining it. After banning one student from attending an interracial meeting at Atlanta University, he shifted course and invited liberal speakers to campus and provided strong support for the YWCA's Institute of Human Relations. The IHR events supplied a steady stream of liberal and radical speakers for at least three years. Shifting course again, he proposed renaming the YWCA to eliminate "YWCA" altogether (as did President McCain of Agnes Scott College) and interrogated YWCA leaders about their attendance at interracial meetings. During this time he hired two resident secretaries who each served only about a year. His middle-of-the-road position was evident when he became frustrated by the difficulty of hiring a politically moderate secretary. In the latter years of the decade, President Wells's vacillation continued. In 1938, he attended a conference sponsored by supporters of Roosevelt's New Deal with the campus YWCA president and hired a history professor known for his support of civil rights activity. Shifting course yet again, in the spring of 1939 he issued a total ban on student attendance at interracial gatherings, eliminating young white women's opportunities to interact with young black men on equal footing.

President Wells's One-Student Ban and His Counteraction

In October 1936, four months after Moss resigned, President Wells for the first time barred a student from attending an interracial meeting. He barred Myra Jenkins from attending a YWCA Southern Regional Council meeting at Atlanta University. Jenkins was a strong leader and served on the YWCA's Southern Regional Council alongside Jane Cassels and on the 1937 Blue Ridge Committee for the summer conference. Atlanta University YMCA-YWCA students were heavily involved in race reform efforts, especially in the interracial discussion groups of the 1920s. The report of the meeting reflected the following: "The chairman read a letter from Myra Jenkins explaining her absence from the council meeting, because of the unwillingness of the college administration to have her attend an interracial meeting at Atlanta University."[1] YWCA national staff blamed white liberal college administrators such as President Wells and President McCain at Agnes Scott College for the decrease in white participation in YWCA race reform efforts across the Southeast. They noted that the shrinking num-

---

[1] "Minutes of the Southern Regional Council, Y.W.C.A., Atlanta University," October 2 to October 4, 1936, Anton files in author's possession.

bers of white students in the mid- to late-1930s and into the 1940s were "largely due to the growing restrictions upon attendance at meetings caused either by official regulation, or by the sense of fear on the part of the administrators."[2]

As if to counteract his banning of Jenkins from the Atlanta University council meeting, President Wells invited several liberal speakers to campus: one in November and two in December. The first was John Curtis Dixon, director of rural education for the Rosenwald Fund. Wells invited Dixon to meet with members of the YWCA, at their request, and speak with them about social problems regarding race and economics. In addition to working for the Rosenwald Fund, Dixon also served as the supervisor of the Division of Negro Education for the State of Georgia (1932 to 1946). In a letter dated November 24, 1936, President Wells wrote:

> The girls of the Y.W.C.A. here are studying two or three problems this year—one that of the tenant farmer from the economic and the educational aspect. They have asked me to invite you to discuss the educational aspect of the negro [sic] problem for them in Chapel some morning for the whole student body.
>
> Every Friday is student day in Chapel. It would be more convenient, therefore, if you could come on Friday of some week. Come down the night before and stay with us. They should also like for you to meet with them in small groups so that they could ask you questions on the problem.[3]

---

[2] Rose Mae Withers, "National Student Staff Annual Report, 1942–1943," August 2, 1943, box 2, reel 144, microdex 4, MS324, Smith College Special Collections.

[3] President Wells to Mr. J. C. Dixon, November 24, 1936, Office of the President, Guy H. Wells, 1936–1937, box 2, folder 5, "Visitors-Past," Special Collections, Georgia College.

Inviting someone associated with the Rosenwald Fund was risky, but especially so since Governor Talmadge frequently pilloried the organization. Plus, President Wells was on thin ice already, given the fall-out of the trip to Fort Valley. Nevertheless, Dixon visited campus and met with YWCA members. Margaret Garbutt, the YWCA president, reported in *The Colonnade* that the meeting of the YWCA race committee was a follow-up on the information Dixon had presented in chapel.[4] Dixon met with the race committee, even though President Wells had earlier called for the YWCA to cease the work of the committee. Dixon would end up being one of the liberal educators whom Governor Talmadge fired as part of the Cocking-Pittman controversy discussed in chapter 5.

About two weeks later, President Wells invited another prominent liberal to campus: George Washington Carver. Recall that historian Delma Presley theorized that President Wells was transferred to Georgia State College for Women from South Georgia Teachers College as punishment for his liberal values on race. One way he expressed those values was arranging speaking events with Carver to travel to audiences across the state. If Presley's theory is true, inviting Carver to GSCW was also risky. In President Wells's December 10, 1936, invitation he reminded Carver of the talk he gave while he was at SGTC, "Cooperating with God." The president invited him to GSCW and offered to arrange for him to speak in Athens (presumably UGA) and at Agnes Scott College. He knew Carver was ill but hoped he would be able to travel. Carver politely declined the invitation and responded, "I fear that it will be impossible for me to do much else than that of being ready for the many demands that are being made upon my time and strength. I shall,

---

[4] "Through the Week with the Y," *The Colonnade* (March 6, 1937): 3.

however, keep in touch with you in the early spring. If at all possible I should like to go to the places you suggest."[5]

President Wells continued to reach out to Rosenwald Fund associates. A few weeks later, in a letter dated December 17, 1936, President Wells wrote Edwin R. Embree, president of the Rosenwald Fund. Embree had written what appeared to be a form letter to President Wells one week earlier and asked for recommendations for students who might qualify to receive Rosenwald fellowships. President Wells responded to Embree: "I appreciate very much the decision of your foundation to offer certain fellowships for the development of unusually talented people in the South, both negroes [*sic*] and whites. I can think of no more far-reaching and worthwhile service that money could be used for than this." He continued, "I want to say that I appreciate very much what you are doing at Statesboro. I worked in that situation for several years and know something of the opportunities." SGTC had received a significant amount of Rosenwald funds and had granted scholarships to many students. At SGTC, President Pittman worked hard to acquire those funds and to develop strong relationships with Rosenwald Fund administrators. In addition to firing John Curtis Dixon, Governor Talmadge also fired President Pittman (discussed in chapter 5). The firings were yet to come, but President Wells was no doubt aware of Governor Talmadge's invectives against the administrators of the Rosenwald Fund. He also, to be sure, held in recent memory the Americanism Committee's critique of the Rosenwald Fund. Nevertheless, he concluded his letter with an invitation to Embree: "I would appreciate your coming to see us sometime and talking over some of our problems with

---

[5] George Washington Carver to President Wells, December 12, 1936, Office of the President, Guy H. Wells 1936–1937, H–Z, box 2, Special Collections, Georgia College.

us."[6] There is no record of a response from Embree, that he ever visited GSCW, or that GSCW received Rosenwald funds.

Inviting More Speakers, Some Liberal, Some Radical: The Institute of Human Relations

In January of 1937, the parade of guest speakers continued. YWCA students organized the first Institute of Human Relations (IHR), and President Wells was all for it. Historian Erica Whittington noted that during the 1940s and 1950s, Southern students committed to race reform often used the term "human relations as code for race relations...when segregation was enforced by rule of law" and that the goals of many YWCA and YMCA campus groups overlapped with the efforts of those organizing "human relations" events.[7] This was true at GSCW.

The first institute was cosponsored with the College Government Association and the Recreation Association. The theme was "Student Responsibilities in Social Change."[8] In an editorial appearing in *The Colonnade*, the author identified the institute as an opportunity for "'Changing Horizons.' This, we interpret to mean a broadening of intellectual horizons, an enlarging of concepts of social change. The problems to be treated during the institute are not remote and vague....[T]hey are concrete, they are present in our own South, they are Georgia's problems, which makes them ours...ours now to consider, ours in a few years to participate in."[9] At every institute, students had

---

[6] President Wells to Edwin R. Embree, December 17, 1936, Office of the President, Guy H. Wells, 1936–1937, H–Z, box 1, folder "Rosenwald, Julius–Fund," Special Collections, Georgia College.

[7] Whittington, "Interracial Dialogue," 84–85.

[8] "Gay Shepperson Heads Four Day Program," *The Colonnade* (January 16, 1937): 1.

[9] "Changing Horizons," *The Colonnade* (January 22, 1937): 2.

the opportunity to arrange individual appointments with the speakers.

The first institute hosted Agnes Scott College sociologist Arthur Raper, author of two highly praised books about race and economics in the South: *The Tragedy of Lynching* published in 1933 and *Preface to Peasantry* published in 1936. He visited two classes, "Contemporary Georgia Problems," typically taught by historian Amanda Johnson, and "Rural Sociology," and he spoke at the institute on "Who Farms in the South?" Historian Fitzhugh Brundage saw Raper as part of a new breed of progressive Southern sociologists devoted to the study of racial oppression.[10] The title of the 1938 institute was "Towards a New Citizenship." Surprisingly, as he was not a progressive governor, Eurith D. Rivers gave the opening address. Radical Southerner Howard Kester spoke on "Regional Problems of the South" and "Labor and Farm Tenancy."[11]

The theme of the January 1939 institute was "Southern Problems." *The Colonnade* reported that "among the most forward thinking Southerns [*sic*] men who have made a life study of the problems of the South were brought to the campus to help students see the questions that they must help solve, and some of the ways in which they may be solved."[12] Myles Horton spoke twice at the institute. He titled one talk "Bread and Soses [*sic*][13] for Workers" and the other, "Democracy for Workers."

---

[10] Brundage, *Lynching in the New South*, 218.

[11] *The Colonnade* (January 22, 1938): 1. Program, the second annual Institute of Human Relations, January 27 to 30, 1938. Office of the President, Guy H. Wells, 1937–1938, C–Z, box 2, folder "IHR," Special Collections, Georgia College.

[12] "IHR Acclaimed 'One of GSC's Best Activities," *The Colonnade* (June 3, 1939): 6.

[13] The title should read "Bread and Roses." Wikipedia, "Bread and Roses," accessed July 26, 2018, https://en.wikipedia.org/wiki/Bread_and_Roses. The

Herman C. Nixon also spoke. Nixon was the author of *Forty Acres and Steel Mules*, a book about the battle between "mechanical agriculture" and the "small farmer," where the small farmer was losing out and living in "sharecropper shacks" in "rural slums." Martha Glad published a review of the book in *The Colonnade* and wrote that Nixon argued that "poverty, illiteracy, and race relations are more closely related than the majority are willing to admit."[14]

From 1937 to 1942, through the IHR, the campus YWCA hosted a steady stream of well-known, liberal, and radical speakers, some of whom critiqued the economic system of capitalism as a system of racial oppression. The plight of poor farmers and sharecroppers of all races were at the center of their analyses, and President Wells fully supported these events. Bringing these speakers to campus for a four-day event with printed programs that included photographs of and information about the speakers as well as a detailed schedule of the four-day event could not have been cheap.[15] In 1940, however, *The Colonnade* editorialized that although the institutes had become a "worthy tradition," they were sometimes not well attended. The editors urged students "to show appreciation to those who strive

---

term "bread and roses" refers to a speech by labor activist Rose Schneiderman in which she argues that workers should earn enough money for both bread and roses. It is often associated with the textile strike in Lawrence, Massachusetts, in 1912.

[14] Martha Glad, "Forty Acres and Steel Mules," *The Colonnade* (February 18, 1939): 6.

[15] "Towards a New Citizenship," program for the second annual Institute of Human Relations, January 27–30, 1938, Office of the President, Guy H. Wells, 1937–1938, C–Z, box 2, folder "Institute of Human Relations;" "Southern Problems," program for the third annual Institute of Human Relations, January 26–29, 1939, Office of the President, Guy H. Wells, 1938–1939, H–Z, box 1, folder "Institute of Human Relations," Special Collections, Georgia College.

to bring worth-while speakers to the campus; to indicate that we are interested in things other than coiffures, clothes, and current boy-friends; and to increase our knowledge of the factors that will greatly influence our lives during and after college."[16]

The occasional sparsely attended IHR did not keep President Wells from inviting another prominent liberal to campus: Frank Graham, president of the University of North Carolina at Chapel Hill. He was unable to speak at the event, but President Wells wrote in his invitation, "The girls are so eager to have you as their main speaker."[17] Graham was known around the South and beyond as a strong advocate for liberal causes. From March 1949 to November 1950, he served as United States senator for North Carolina to complete J. Melville Broughton's term, who died in office. President Franklin D. Roosevelt appointed Graham to serve on several New Deal committees, and he served for almost two years as president of the left-leaning and socialist-inspired Southern Conference for Human Welfare.

Renaming

President Wells solidified his pattern of uneven support for the YWCA in the last few years of the 1930s. He offered strong support to the YWCA's IHR events, but at the same time suggested to Chancellor Sanford that the name "YWCA" be changed to "Religious Activities." This gesture could be interpreted as support, or at least protection from scrutiny. But given

[16] "Institute of Human Relations Has Become A Worthy Tradition," *The Colonnade* (January 20, 1940): 2.

[17] President Wells to Frank Graham, n.d., but is likely to have been mailed the summer of 1939, Office of the President, Guy H. Wells, 1939–1940, A–L, box 3, folder "Institute of Human Relations," Special Collections, Georgia College.

the YWCA's response to a similar effort by President McCain of Agnes Scott College, the YWCA saw the move as hostile. Nevertheless, President Wells suggested the name change after he received a letter from an Atlanta alumni association whose members attacked the YWCA's interracial activities and were convinced that the organization was Moscow-directed and infiltrated by the Rosenwald-funded American Civil Liberties Union (ACLU).

In November of 1937, the Atlanta Alumnae Association of GSCW wrote to President Wells with two objections. One, they objected to President Wells's consideration of a woman for a dean's position without a degree from a "Standard College," as they put it. Second, and more important for the purposes of this book, they "object[ed] to the activities of the Y.W.C.A. on the race question, and urgently request[ed] that the college see that the girls are not permitted to attend inter-racial gatherings." Along with their letter they included a three-page, typewritten document titled "The Soviet Hand in Georgia." Members of the ACLU, association members wrote, contacted "college professors, preachers, church officials, Y.M.C.A. and Y.W.C.A. groups" to infiltrate them while they drew a salary from the Rosenwald Fund. The association claimed that if (white) people were not vigilant that before long "you will see Moscow-directed student organizations talking the language of the bolshevicks [sic] and promoting interracial programs" and "racial equality."[18]

It is impossible to know if the letter from alumni caused President Wells to suggest to Chancellor Sanford that the YWCA change its name to "Religious Activities." But his sug-

---

[18] Atlanta Alumnae Association of GSCW to President Wells, November 15, 1937, Office of the President, Guy H. Wells, 1938–1939, Special Collections, Georgia College.

gestion nonetheless revealed his political acumen. On March 9, 1938, the president wrote to the chancellor:

> Sometime ago in a conversation with me you said you thought the time had come for us to abolish the Y.W.C.A.... I should like to suggest an alternative plan for our situation here—that you allow us to change the large organization to the name of Religious Activities, and that the secretary of the Y.W.C.A. be called the secretary of Religious Activities.... I think this plan would keep us from getting the backfire of criticism which we get now, and which you, no doubt, wish to correct.[19]

There is no record of Chancellor Sanford's response, and the YWCA kept its name. Five years later, in 1943, a new organization briefly emerged called the "Coordinated Council of Religious Activities" (CCRA), but it was a separate entity, and students voted on the measure; it was not a directive from President Wells.

President McCain Renames the Agnes Scott YWCA

President McCain faced challenges similar to those experienced by President Wells. McCain and Wells were both harassed by Mrs. Andrews and Superior Court Judge James C. Davis of the Stone Mountain Judicial Circuit about their students' YWCA activity. Mrs. Andrews and Judge Davis identified GSCW and Agnes Scott as two places where Communism and social equality were promoted.

It was no coincidence that Mrs. Andrews, the American Legion, and Judge Davis singled out GSCW and Agnes Scott College. These were two white *women's* colleges with active

---

[19] President Wells to Steadman V. Sanford, March 9, 1938, Office of the President, Guy H. Wells, 1938–1939, A–G, box 2, folder 2 "Board of Regents-March 1938," Special Collections, Georgia College.

YWCAs. The YWCA activities that brought the most vigilant surveillance and the harshest censure were those that were likely to have involved or did involve black men, such as the gatherings at Fort Valley N&I and at Atlanta University. Student trips or even planned student trips to black campuses caught the attention of those who kept their eyes on white women and the opportunities they may have had to interact with black men on an equal basis.

The "cult of white Southern womanhood" assumed that white women needed protection from black men and that white men could and should protect them. After slavery ended, stereotypes of black men changed from images of shiftless and lazy to strong and violent. This brutish figure supposedly roamed the countryside looking to rape white women.[20] D. W. Griffith's early 1900s propagandistic novel trilogy about the Ku Klux Klan contributed to this rape myth. Griffith's portrayal of the Klan as a group of heroic white men who protected white women from the savagery and brutality of black men was the focus of his novels and was depicted in the commercially successful 1915 silent film *The Birth of a Nation*. The cult of white Southern womanhood was essential to this myth. The ideology portrayed white women, particularly elite women, as docile, pure, and innocent and in need of protection from the sexual advances of now freed black men. Black women were seen as even lower in the racial and gender hierarchy and as not being worthy of protection.

Mrs. Andrews, Joseph Kamp, and others opposed to civil rights used the cult of white Southern womanhood to their advantage. In her letters to the press and to other college administrators, Mrs. Andrews wrote of a "jungle" of black incivility and

---

[20] See Patricia Hill Collins's *Black Feminist Thought* for a discussion of these controlling images.

wildness that she feared would corrupt white women students at GSCW and Agnes Scott College. Bubbling beneath the surface was their ultimate fear: miscegenation.

Agnes Scott students were very much involved in the YWCA's efforts to dismantle the racial order in the South. In the 1920s, they were active in the first interracial discussion groups in Atlanta organized by Frances Williams and Katharine Du Pre Lumpkin as part of the YWCA's 1919 directive. President McCain's daughters, Louise Irene (class of 1934) and Isabel (class of 1937), were both members of the YWCA at Agnes Scott. Isabel served as president during some of the most public debates regarding the claim that the YWCA was a Communist organization. As president, she celebrated its radical edge and encouraged first-year students to join: "And perhaps you will discover that a real warning is pertinent, because fundamentally the Y.W.C.A. is a dangerous organization. It actually purports to change people and things."[21]

In May of 1937, two years after Judge Davis criticized the GSCW YWCA to President Wells, he wrote President McCain. He asked, "Do you think our young girls are old enough or wise enough to take care of themselves in communist-promoted meetings of mixed races held in basements of a negro [sic] church unchaperoned?"[22] President McCain re-

---

[21] "Freshmen Invited to Join Y.W.C.A. in Year's Program," *Agonextra*, a section of the *Agonistic*, September 22, 1936. The *Agonistic* was the name of the student newspaper of Agnes Scott College from 1916 to 1939. In 1939 the name changed to the *Agnes Scott News*.

[22] James C. Davis, Al Henson, William L. Van Dyke to J.R. McCain, May 3, 1937, Commission on Interracial Cooperation Papers, Anton files in author's possession. Anton shared her files with the authors, which she originally acquired from the Trevor Arnett Library, Atlanta University, now the Archives Research Center, Atlanta University Center, Robert W. Woodruff Library.

sponded: "For more than twenty years—before any of your organizations were concerned about the matter—we have consistently opposed efforts for the social intermingling of the races. It is no new problem with us. We have likewise opposed unceasingly any tendencies toward communism, though we have never found any among our own students."[23] Just as President Wells had done, President McCain avowed that no one on his campus, student or faculty, had advocated for the equality of blacks and whites—that on his campus white supremacy was firmly in place.

After Louise Irene and Isabel graduated and about one year after Judge Davis wrote him, President McCain changed the name of the YWCA at Agnes Scott. This occurred during the same month and year, March of 1938, as President Wells's attempt. Even though "YWCA" no longer appeared in the association's title, the chapter retained its YWCA affiliation. [24] YWCA leaders of the Southern region suspected that President McCain had led YWCA members to believe that this shift in name and organization of the religious associations at Agnes Scott required disaffiliation with the YWCA. They believed that President McCain "was obviously using this indirect method to break affiliation with the national movement and thus rid himself of the increasingly difficult situation in regard to the

---

[23] J. R. McCain to James C. Davis, Al Henson, William. L. Van Dyke, May 6, 1937, Commission on Interracial Cooperation Papers, Anton files in author's possession.

[24] President McCain to Winifred Kellersberger, March 8, 1938, James Ross McCain Papers, "Christian Association–Events & Publicity," Special Collections and Archives, McCain Library, Agnes Scott College, Decatur, GA. Agnes Scott College YWCA leaders, including President Winifred Kellersberger, wrote President McCain informing him of their intentions and included a preamble in their correspondence. President McCain wrote back approving their initiative in a letter addressed to Kellersberger.

participation of representatives of the Association in activities of a racially inclusive Christian organization." [25] President McCain's name change idea immediately materialized, unlike President Wells's. In 1938, the YWCA at Agnes Scott College became the "Agnes Scott Christian Association."[26]

President McCain and President Wells both had to answer to conservative and powerful politicians, judges, and administrators who believed that the YWCA was a "Negro-controlled" and Communist organization run by outsiders from New York City. YWCA leaders may thus have been right that President McCain used the name change to direct critics' attention elsewhere, thereby making his own job easier.

Interrogation

In 1938, President Wells had every reason to want to appease Chancellor Sanford by suggesting he change the name of the campus YWCA to "Religious Activities." That same year the chancellor asked President Wells about another trip to Atlanta University that YWCA students took the year before. On August 26, 1938, after Chancellor Sanford's request for information about the trip, President Wells promptly wrote letters to two students, Margaret Garbutt, the YWCA president for the 1937–1938 academic year, and Marguerite Jernigan, the YWCA president for the 1938–1939 academic year.

President Wells explained to Garbutt that students' attendance at interracial meetings, such as the one in Atlanta the year before, were "going to assume a rather large place this year if I

---

[25] Annual Report, Southern Region National Student Staff, 1937–1938, box 2, reel 144, microdex 4, MS324, Smith College Special Collections.

[26] *Agonistic* (May 11, 1938).

cannot clear it up." He said that "an accusation has been made" to Chancellor Sanford that students attended this meeting at Atlanta University. He wrote to Garbutt that he informed the chancellor that he was sure it wasn't true, "for I had asked the girls not to attend these meetings which some thought were questionable." He explained that if anyone went to this meeting without his permission, "I am in trouble. Please write me all you know about these activities."[27]

President Wells's letter to Marguerite Jernigan was much the same.[28] Jernigan responded and reminded the president that she was incoming president of the YWCA and therefore did not have "full details of everything that happened in the Y last year. So far as I know, however, the only meeting at Atlanta University that any of our students attended was the Blue Ridge Planning Comm[ittee] which Margaret Garbutt went to. I would suggest that you write to Jane Gilmer or to Margaret, if you wish more information." Being politic herself, Jernigan concluded, "I am not surprised that students who try to live Christian lives are questioned in our world today. The Y.W.C.A. is a voluntary religious organization though, and no one is forced to belong and certainly no one is forced to go to any meeting that she doesn't want to attend."[29]

President Wells had written to former resident secretary Jane Gilmer in a letter also dated August 26. President Wells's

---

[27] President Wells to Margaret Garbutt, August 26, 1938, Office of the President, Guy H. Wells, 1937–1938, C–Z, box 3, folder "YWCA," Special Collections, Georgia College.

[28] President Wells to Marguerite Jernigan, August 26, 1938, Office of the President, Guy H. Wells, 1937–1938, C–Z, box 3, folder "YWCA," Special Collections, Georgia College.

[29] Marguerite Jernigan to President Wells, August 31, 1938, Office of the President, Guy H. Wells, 1938–1939, A–C, box 2, folder "Board of Regents-September," Special Collections, Georgia College.

letter to Gilmer was much the same as that written to Jernigan and Garbutt.[30] There is no record of Gilmer's response, as she had left the resident secretary position in 1937 and was likely out of touch, but, like Jernigan, Garbutt responded and implied that she had every right to attend. She referred to the meeting as a business meeting and that she stayed at the Baker Street YWCA, which was for whites only. Mary Jane Willett, student YWCA secretary for the Southern region, explained the living arrangements regarding the meeting Garbutt attended: "Special rates have been secured from Atlanta University for the Leadership Meeting. The majority of persons (Negro and white) can be housed in the Graduate Dormitory at Atlanta University. Additional rooms are available (for Negro and white members of the group) in the Spelman Dormitories on the Atlanta University campus. A limited number of rooms are available at the Baker Street Y.W.C.A. residence (for white members of the group only)."[31] Garbutt stated that she did not eat at the university and her expenses were paid by the National Student Council. She added, "I went to the meeting not as a representative of the G.S.C.W. local Y.W.C.A. but as a member of the National Student Council."[32]

During the last four years of the 1930s, President Wells's support of the YWCA diminished compared to when he first arrived at GSCW. There were moments of support when he

[30] President Wells to Jane Gilmer, August 26, 1938, Office of the President, Guy H. Wells, 1937–1938, C–Z, box 3, folder "YWCA," Special Collections, Georgia College.

[31] Mary Jane Willett, "Living Arrangements," September 23, 1937, informational letter regarding the meeting Garbutt attended, box 2, reel 144, microdex 5, MS324, Smith College Special Collection.

[32] Margaret Garbutt to President Wells, September 3, 1938, Office of the President, Guy H. Wells, 1938–1939, A–C, box 2, folder "Board of Regents September," Special Collections, Georgia College.

got behind their IHR effort and when he invited liberal speakers to campus himself. But the overall feel of his relationship with the YWCA was one of distrust and frustration, which led to an increasing lack of support. Students seemed wary of the president's questioning of their off-campus activities. His own frustration was evident in his effort to hire a more moderate resident secretary to replace Polly Moss.

Searching for a Moderate Resident Secretary

President Wells searched the Southeast for a moderate replacement for Moss. One of the first serious contenders was Florence DeFrees. She was friends with Moss and had worked at Randolph-Macon Woman's College in Lynchburg, Virginia, presumably as the resident secretary. At the time of the application, DeFrees was studying religious education at Columbia University's Teachers College. President Wells was interested in hiring her, but he was concerned that she might not know how to "handle the race question." He wrote several people inquiring as to whether or not she could perform as a moderate, particularly when it came to race, including Dr. Clara W. Davidson, associate professor of religion at Randolph-Macon; Dean C. Clement French of Randolph-Macon; and the president of the college, T. H. Jack. He asked President Jack:

> As perhaps [sic] know, one of the most difficult problems that has developed in the Y program in the South is the race question. I feel that a good many of the Y leaders have an impractical complex on the subject, and I should want to have a thorough understanding on this particular slant before considering Miss DeFrees. I realize that there is a distinct race problem, and I want our students to become conscious of it. I do not agree that we can go the whole distance some of the Y leaders have advocated. Certainly a school

supported with public money cannot sponsor extreme liberalism. Some of the leaders also have an extreme bias on pacifism. This matter does not worry me very much, because I am somewhat of a pacifist myself, not to the extent that I would never go to war, however. I am mentioning these things, because you will be able to give me light on these points in your reply.[33]

In a separate letter President Wells informed Dean French that teachers at Randolph-Macon said that DeFrees was asked to leave Randolph-Macon "because of her inability to handle the race problem there."[34] Dean French responded on behalf of President Jack and explained that President Jack was ill. He said that DeFrees left Randolph-Macon of her own accord and was not asked to leave for any reason, including the so-called inability to handle the race problem.[35]

In addition to DeFrees, there were twenty-six other applicants for the resident secretary position. Southern Regional Secretary Mary Jane Willett and other national YWCA leaders recommended a total of nine applicants, none of whom the president selected. Instead, he hired Mary Elizabeth Dale, who began her duties in September of 1937. The author of the YWCA annual report stated that President Wells hired Dale "because she knew nothing about the Y.W.C.A." and concluded that hiring Dale was a sign of how the association at GSCW

---

[33] President Wells to T. H. Jack, February 26, 1937, Office of the President, Guy H. Wells, 1938–1939, A–G, box 2, Special Collections, Georgia College.

[34] President Wells to C. Clement French, March 29, 1937, Office of the President, Guy H. Wells, 1938–1939, A–G, box 2, Special Collections, Georgia College.

[35] C. Clement French to President Wells, March 31, 1937, Office of the President, Guy H. Wells, 1938–1939, A–G, box 2, Special Collections, Georgia College.

"continues to struggle against administrative and political restrictions to their participation in intercollegiate and racially inclusive activities of the movement in Georgia." In fact, the report stated that Dale felt that Wells misrepresented the position
to her "as one of general director of religious activities and
teacher of religion." The report concluded, "In face of steady
opposition to the Y.W.C.A. program from the administration
and the state legislature, it is more than likely that the Association and the new secretary will have an unusually difficult time
next year."[36] Dale held the position for one year. Once she resigned, President Wells hired Jane Gilmer, but she also left the
position soon after she was hired.

By May of 1938, President Wells still had not found a
YWCA resident secretary to replace Mary Elizabeth Dale and
Jane Gilmer. Dale and Gilmer had each served as resident secretaries for no more than a year. President Wells wrote to
Chancellor O. C. Carmichael of Vanderbilt that he wanted to
take special care to hire someone who was liberal but "sanely
so."[37] In August, he wrote to Dean Adams, who was in New
York City at the time, that he was "more lost than ever" in his
search. He asked if she would visit Union Theological Seminary
and the Teachers College at Columbia and interview any students the staff there might recommend. Wells described his
ideal secretary:

> I am not going to approve any narrow, short-sighted, reli-
> gious fanatic for the place, if I know it. I had rather go
> without a person than to get the wrong one. There are peo-

---

[36] Annual Report, 1937–1938, box 2, reel 144, microdex 4, MS324,
Smith College Special Collection.

[37] President Wells to O. C. Carmichael, May 2, 1938, Office of the
President, Guy H. Wells, 1938–1939, A–G, box 1, folder "Applications-
Social Sciences," Special Collections, Georgia College.

ple in the town here that are going to embarrass me if I don't find a person. There are some church people that would like to put in somebody that they think would be all right, but which I know would not have a religious program for our day and generation. I have had a little flurry of newspaper publicity about a recent nomination of mine to the History Department [Dr. Mack Swearingen]. I have enough trouble with the normal run or [sic] things without getting into more trouble with the "Y" and this religious work. I realize the world must have some radicals. I also know that the great majority of people must learn the lessons of conservation as well as the discovery of new ideals.[38]

President Wells's letter revealed that he thought moderation was best.

Despite the high turnover of resident secretaries, the race committee was still active, and members studied and published articles in *The Colonnade* about the plight of German refugees, peace, propaganda, and a possible federal minimum wage. Their time without a long-term resident secretary ended in 1939, however, when President Wells hired Cynthia Mallory. Mallory would serve as secretary until 1943. While not as progressive as Goodson and Moss, Mallory established Religious Emphasis Week in 1940, which continued the steady stream of liberal and radical campus speakers.

Hiring a Liberal Professor and the Southern Conference for Human Welfare

President Wells's frustrated interrogation of YWCA leaders Garbutt and Jernigan and his search for a moderate replacement

---

[38] President Wells to Ethel Adams, August 9, 1938, Office of the President, Guy H. Wells, 1938–1939, box 2, folder "Application-Y Secretary," Special Collections, Georgia College.

for Moss could only mean he was about to move toward the left: he hired a liberal history professor and went with the professor and the YWCA college president to the inaugural left-leaning Southern Conference for Human Welfare.

On August 9, 1938, a headline in the Macon *Telegraph* read "LIBERAL TEACHER HIRED BY GSCW." President Wells had proposed the hiring of Mack Swearingen of Tulane University, whose administrators had charged him with "subversive activities against the United States government." Historian William Ivy Hair explained that "these charges stemmed from two activities: he had presided over a meeting of 'Friends of Democratic Spain' (an anti-Franco group); and was a member of a committee which protested to the mayor of New Orleans over the arrests of alleged 'communists' in New Orleans— one of those arrested being the secretary of the New Orleans YWCA." Swearingen was acquitted but wanted to leave Tulane. Before the board of regents had confirmed his hire at GSCW, which was usually a simple formality, local newspapers had gotten wind of the history professor's controversial past. Hair reported that "there was considerable pressure on the board not to hire Swearingen. Letters questioning the appointment came from various organizations, including locals of the American Legion, Veterans of Foreign Wars, the United Spanish War Veterans. And Mrs. J. E. Andrews." After the board of regents investigated Swearingen, they approved his hiring in October of 1938.[39]

Swearingen was an active faculty member at GSCW. He served as head of the history department, participated in campus debates, spoke at YWCA events, and was a frequent contributor to *The Colonnade*. He often wrote articles appearing in the col-

---

[39] Hair et al., *A Centennial History*, 199, 200.

umn "It Looks From Here." In the fall of 1936, *The Colonnade* won a state award for the column that included "commentary on significant national and international news of the week or a short article on problems of the South."[40] Swearingen was one of the many faculty members whom President Wells hired who was not a native of Georgia. Governor Talmadge targeted and shamed non-native Georgians, or "foreigners," as he labeled them, so for President Wells to hire a non-native after the Fort Valley trip was risky, even though the board of regents approved his hiring.

Another move toward the left was President Wells's attendance at the 1938 inaugural Southern Conference for Human Welfare (SCHW), organized by "liberal southern New Dealers" in November, in Birmingham, Alabama.[41] Swearingen and President Wells attended with their wives, along with the campus YWCA president, Marguerite Jernigan. First Lady Eleanor Roosevelt also attended the event as well as Supreme Court Justice Hugo Black. The SCHW, according to historian David Chappell, was an organization that wanted to make political change in the South on the basis of corralling political power, not moral power, and this first meeting in Birmingham was an effort to begin such a strategy. The gathering had the "official blessing" of the Communist Party of the USA, although the party played a limited role in the meeting.[42] At the first gathering, the SCHW focused on combatting Jim Crow segregation and poll taxes.[43] Historian Robin D. G. Kelley described the conference as "a rousing success" with more than

---

[40] "Press Bulletin Praises Column," *The Colonnade* (November 21, 1936): 1.

[41] Lovett, *The Civil Rights Movement in Tennessee*, 6.

[42] Kelley, *Hammer and Hoe*, 166–67.

[43] Lovett, *The Civil Rights Movement in Tennessee*, 416.

twelve hundred attendees. In addition to Eleanor Roosevelt and Hugo Black, University of North Carolina president Frank Graham presided as president of the organization, and also in attendance were Myles Horton, Mary McLeod Bethune, Benjamin Mays, and Herman C. Nixon.[44] A frequent speaker at GSCW, Nixon was also president of the SCHW and former head of the Department of Sociology at Tulane.[45] (He was probably familiar with Mack Swearingen.)

The first day of the meeting was integrated with about one thousand participants, a quarter of whom were black.[46] On the second day of the meeting, then city commissioner Theophilus Eugene "Bull" Connor ordered segregated seating. First Lady Eleanor Roosevelt protested by sitting with blacks and then sitting in the aisle.[47] Supporters and leaders of the organization were seen as "un-American" and advocates of Communism if not Communists themselves. Soon after the conference, Swearingen defended his attendance in a *Colonnade* article. He said the conference had been unfairly labeled as "un-American."[48] In 1942, after an active four years at GSCW, which included strong support of the campus YWCA, Swearingen took a position at Elmira College, a women's college in New York.[49] There is no record that he was forced to leave GSCW.

---

[44] Kelley, *Hammer and Hoe*, 185; Lovett, *The Civil Rights Movement in Tennessee*, 6.

[45] "Y' Column," *The Colonnade* (November 12, 1938): 4.

[46] Egerton, *Speak Now Against the Day*, 297.

[47] Lovett, *The Civil Rights Movement in Tennessee*, 6.

[48] Mack Swearingen, "It Looks From Here," *The Colonnade* (December 3, 1938): 3, 8.

[49] Hair et al., *A Centennial History*, 201.

A Total Ban on Interracial Gatherings

As part of his strategy of playing the middle, President Wells provided uneven support of the campus YWCA and their interracial activities. He hired Mack Swearingen, who became a YWCA advocate, and then he attended the SCHW in Birmingham with Swearingen and YWCA president Marguerite Jernigan. A few months later, in early 1939, in a countermove, President Wells banned all YWCA students from attending the black student conferences at Kings Mountain. Under the delegate system, black delegates attended the white students' conference and vice versa.

President Wells then banned GSCW students from attending *any* interracial conferences. Someone anonymously responded to President Wells's delegate restrictions in an April 8, 1939, opinion piece in *The Colonnade*. The title of the piece was "Does Non-Attendance at Mixed Confabs [interracial conferences] Strengthen 'White Supremacy?'" The author criticized the ruling that no GSCW delegate could attend a YWCA interracial student conference and proclaimed that "such a situation is one that should not exist at an alleged institution of higher learning." Later that same year, Jernigan, the campus YWCA president in 1938–1939, spoke frankly in her annual report. She expressed her disappointment in GSCW and the USG administration: "We have been severely handicapped...by the fact that the administration of G.S.C.W. and of the University System would not grant us permission to attend any interracial conferences at all. This has meant that we have not been able to attend any Y conferences." She also stated that much "damage" had been done because without connections to others outside GSCW, students lose "a sense of kindredship with people throughout the world who are working for a better world of liberty, justice, peace, and brotherly love. It is absolutely essential that some definite action be taken next year toward working out an understanding with the Administration and the Board of Regents which will enable us to attend Y.W.C.A. meetings."[50]

In October of 1939, four months after she wrote her annual report, Jernigan described the YWCA as a campus association riddled with problems: "lack of money for conferences; officers not realizing their responsibilities; no calendar for scheduled meetings; lack of interest, knowledge, and understanding."[51] Given that Milledgeville was geographically isolated, restricting students' travel to conferences created an overall lack of enthusiasm for YWCA activity. It was no help that since Moss resigned there had been a high turnover of resident secretaries, and Jernigan appeared to have little confidence in the new secretary, Cynthia Mallory.

After President Wells banned GSCW students from attending interracial conferences, he asked Marion Smith, chair of the board of regents, about similar YWCA activities at the University of Georgia. Smith assured President Wells that based on his conversation with President Harmon Caldwell, nothing of the sort had happened at UGA. Smith stated the board's position on the matter:

> Regardless of all theoretical or abstract views about inter-racial relations, actually inter-racial student conferences on this subject in Georgia at the present time are unwise in the most extreme degree. We will support the heads of institutions in taking whatever steps they may deem to be necessary to control the crack-brain element of YMCA and

---

[50] "Annual Report of the President of Y.W.C.A.," June 3, 1939, Office of the President, Guy H. Wells, 1938–1939, H–Z, box 2, Special Collections, Georgia College.

[51] "Poll of Student Interest Helps 'Y' Meet Problems," *The Colonnade* (October 7, 1939): 1.

YWCA workers and to prevent such inter-racial student conferences occurring so far as the students of their institution are concerned.[52]

President Wells responded, "We have kept our students from attending these meetings and expect to do so.... This is no new trouble with us. The Y group seems to be dominated by northern leaders who do not understand the situation in the South. Atlanta University seems to be the center from which they do their work."[53]

This was not the first time President Wells took sides against the YWCA and with USG administration. As this chapter demonstrated, President Wells found numerous ways to side with the conservative forces of the state. Yet as this chapter also demonstrated, President Wells did not leave the YWCA completely behind. His inconsistent support allowed it to stay up and running, even if students' activities were significantly curtailed. But brighter days were ahead. Helen Matthews Lewis referred to these brighter days as "a small period of safe space for progressive change in Georgia."[54]

---

[52] Marion Smith to President Wells, October 10, 1939, Office of the President, Guy H. Wells, 1938–1939, Special Collections, Georgia College.

[53] President Wells to Marion Smith, October 12, 1939, Office of the President, Guy H. Wells, 1938–1939, Special Collections, Georgia College.

[54] Lewis, "GSCW in the 1940s," 50.

Chapter 5

Lesson Three:
Move Left Under Liberal Governors

The USG Cocking-Pittman controversy of 1941 played a major role in the election of Ellis Arnall as governor in 1942 and created openings for progressive change in Georgia. The election of Arnall and the distraction from routine caused by World War II allowed President Wells to shift to a more flexible approach to overseeing the YWCA. He lifted the ban on student attendance at interracial gatherings and hired a dynamic new resident secretary, Emily Cottingham.

Cottingham served as secretary on a crowded campus as World War II brought to GSCW women training for the Women's Auxiliary Volunteer Enlisted Service (WAVES). The war also brought jobs for many women across the country still struggling with economic hardship following the Great Depression. Civil rights work was energized as black soldiers began to speak out against segregation in the military. The war, the USG Cocking-Pittman controversy, and the election of Ellis Arnall helped open a space for the passage of progressive legislation in Georgia such as the abolishment of the poll tax. All of these events decreased the hold of Eugene Talmadge populism, which historian Patrick Novotny defined as "an amalgam of racism, isolationism in international affairs, and a suspicion of those whom he considered to be outsiders or 'foreigners,' as he termed those born outside Georgia."[1] Toward the end of the decade, when the Talmadge dynasty reemerged, there had been enough legislative change in Georgia to weaken the dynasty. But by that time, President Wells had set his sights beyond GSCW.

Openings for Progressive Change:
The Cocking-Pittman Controversy
and World War II

Historian Glenda Gilmore summarized Governor Talmadge's inquisition against liberal educators: "Back in the governor's office in Georgia after four years of sulking and criticizing FDR, [Talmadge] went on a tear in 1941, abolishing the offices of the controller general and state treasurer, burning books, and announcing that he would fire any university professor who 'dissents from the proposition that the white man is by nature the superior of the black man.'"[2] Two university educators at the top of his list of targets were Dean Walter D. Cocking and President Marvin S. Pittman.

The Southern regional secretaries of the student YWCA knew about Governor Talmadge's rampage and mentioned him by name. In their annual report for 1940–1941, Augusta Roberts and Celestine Smith wrote of two events that were of particular significance for their work that year: "Developing tensions and war hysteria as evidenced in state sponsored alien and red-bating [sic], and increased curtailment of civil liberties." They added that "in several centers in the South and in the

---

[1] Novotny, *This Georgia Rising*, 8.
[2] Gilmore, *Defying Dixie*, 351.

State of Georgia in particular there has been increased racial tension created largely by reactionary political leadership."[3]

At the May 30, 1941, meeting of the USG Board of Regents, Governor Talmadge claimed that Dean Cocking had "violated Southern traditions" and "said things contrary to Southern principles." The governor referred to a statement he claimed Dean Cocking had made "that he wanted to see the time when a school for Negroes would be established in Athens so that Negroes and white boys and girls could associate together."[4]

Sylla Hamilton made the charges. Hamilton was a teacher in the Practice School of the Coordinate College, part of UGA, and under the supervision of Dean Cocking. The director at Hamilton's school had recommended her dismissal apparently in an effort to raise the quality of teachers, and Dean Cocking had complied. After her firing, she accused the dean of supporting integration. She claimed he had made such statements at a staff meeting of the College of Education on March 31, 1939.

Governor Talmadge appointed Chair of the Board of Regents Sandy Beaver to investigate. Beaver collected sworn statements from Sylla Hamilton; Dean Preston Brooks, her boss at her new job at the Institute for the Study of Georgia Problems, where she was moved after the firing; Professor Horace B. Ritchie, Cocking's assistant; Dean Cocking; University System chancellor Steadman V. Sanford; and UGA president Harmon W. Caldwell. After discussing the situation with these individuals, Beaver concluded that Hamilton's charges were un-

---

[3] Augusta Roberts and Celestine Smith, "National Student Staff Annual Report, 1940–1941," July 2, 1941, box 2, reel 144, microdex 4, MS324, Smith College Special Collections.

[4] Novotny, *This Georgia Rising*, 46, 54.

substantiated and reported such to Governor Talmadge.[5] Ignoring Sandy Beaver's recommendation, Governor Talmadge sided with Hamilton and accused Dean Cocking of supporting integration and Communism. At the meeting, Governor Talmadge acted on his declaration "that he would ask the board of regents to remove 'any person in the university system advocating Communism or racial equality.'"[6] According to Governor Talmadge, Dean Cocking was one of those persons.

Walter Dewey Cocking was born in Iowa and educated at Columbia University. For Governor Talmadge, this marked Cocking as unfit for his role as dean, despite his experience as an administrator in Iowa, Texas, and Missouri, despite serving as professor of school administration at George Peabody College for Teachers in Nashville, Tennessee, and despite serving as commissioner of education for Tennessee from 1933 to 1937.[7] During the board of regents controversy, Governor Talmadge noted that in Iowa "the racial question is not the same as it is in Georgia," suggesting that Dean Cocking, as an outsider, could not properly understand Georgia racial dynamics.[8]

Also, at the May 30 meeting, Governor Talmadge accused Marvin S. Pittman, president of Georgia Teachers College (the name changed from South Georgia Teachers College to Georgia Teachers College in 1939) of the same offenses as those he had accused Dean Cocking of, in addition to Pittman having

---

[5] Bailes, "Eugene Talmadge and the Board of Regents Controversy," 410.

[6] Novotny, *This Georgia Rising*, 46–47.

[7] New Georgia Encyclopedia, "Cocking Affair," last modified November 8, 2013, https://www.georgiaencyclopedia.org/articles/government-politics/cocking-affair.

[8] Bailes, "Eugene Talmadge and the Board of Regents Controversy," 412.

"too enthusiastic an interest in politics."[9] Governor Talmadge alleged that Pittman had removed campaign banners from the Bulloch County Courthouse where he held a rally on August 20, 1940, and prevented college students from attending a speech of Talmadge's in downtown Statesboro, all of which President Pittman denied. Like Dean Cocking, President Pittman was educated at Columbia University. Before earning his PhD from Columbia Teachers College, he earned his master's degree at the University of Oregon. Immediately prior to taking the position of president at GTC, he had served as director of laboratory schools and teacher training at Michigan State Normal School.[10] President Pittman's Southern birth (in Mississippi), however, did not protect him from being on Governor Talmadge's "foreigner" hit list.

At the May 30, 1941, meeting, the board of regents voted eight to four, with Chair Sandy Beaver abstaining, to dismiss Dean Cocking and President Pittman. The board recessed for a little over an hour, during which time Harmon Caldwell was notified of the action taken and communicated to Sandy Beaver that he would resign if the board did not provide Dean Cocking with a proper hearing (President Pittman was not under his supervision). When the meeting resumed, Governor Talmadge and Chair Beaver argued. The board then rescinded its action and allowed a hearing, which was scheduled for June 10. Students demonstrated to show support for President Pittman. Statesboro citizens also showed strong support, and Dean Cocking was supported as well. Making a big fuss and creating a spectacle, Governor Talmadge ordered investigations of "anti-American" books and requested the dismissal of Sandy Beaver.

[9] Novotny, *This Georgia Rising*, 46.
[10] Altman, "Marvin S. Pittman," 2.

And on July 14, 1941, the board of regents voted, ten to five, to remove Dean Cocking and President Pittman.[11]

After the board of regents voted to oust Dean Cocking and President Pittman, President Wells was concerned about losing his own position. After all, he had allowed the Rosenwald Fund's J. C. Dixon to speak to students at chapel about the problems of education facing blacks, he had caught the governor's attention thanks to the "wild" trip to Fort Valley, he had hired "known liberal" and non-native Mack Swearingen, he had attended the Southern Conference for Human Welfare, and, prior to coming to GSCW, he had worked with his African American colleague and president of Georgia State Industrial College, Benjamin F. Hubert, to bring George Washington Carver to campuses across the state. President Wells wrote to his attorney friend Howell Cone on August 4, 1941, that he feared he would be fired. Two weeks later Cone responded:

> I am beginning to think you are really worried about your situation. I had thought you were magnifying the dangers, as I cannot think you are seriously threatened. In my view, unless there has been a plan already for further "purges" or else some flagrant outbreak occurs, it is rather late for any further "liquidation." In fact, I am inclined now to think that the Board of Regents are rather anxious for matters to quiet down, that is the majority of them—the ten. I think they have begun to believe that already they have gone too far, which is a correct viewpoint. So, if I were you, I would quit worrying about your place there.[12]

As it turned out, the trouble that lay ahead was not the loss of President Wells's job, but the loss of GSCW's accreditation.

---

[11] Novotny, *This Georgia Rising*, 57, 64, 67.

[12] Howell Cone to President Wells, August 18, 1941, Office of the President, Guy H. Wells, 1940–1941, C–Z, box 1, folder "Howell Cone," Special Collections, Georgia College.

On July 16, 1941, two days after the board of regents voted to oust Dean Cocking and President Pittman, the Southern Association of Colleges and Secondary Schools (SACSS) announced that it would investigate the dismissals.[13] Georgia college students from across the state organized, including students from GSCW. On the front page of *The Colonnade* the headline read: "GSCW Joins to Save University System."[14] In the middle of the page, offset in a large box with the title "This Will Happen To Us," appeared a list of fourteen consequences of the loss of accreditation such as "No teacher receiving her degree from a State college can teach in a Georgia accredited school." Also appearing on the front page was an appeal from the campus YWCA president, Mary Jeanne Everett: "We cannot take the fight half-heartedly but must enter into it 'heart and soul' if we would see our aims accomplished.... And so I challenge every GSCW girl—every Y member—every Georgia student to give our first push together with great force and so proving that we are not complacent, apathetic, and indifferent to our future and the future of Georgia education." On October 25, 1941, the *Atlanta Constitution* reported on the front page that "1000 G.S.C.W. Students Ask Legislature to 'Curb' Governor."

Despite the protests of students, faculty, and community members, however, on December 4, 1941, all of Georgia's state-supported colleges for whites lost their accreditation for one year. On December 6, *The Colonnade* listed the following schools as having lost accreditation: UGA, Georgia Tech, GSCW, GSWC, GTC, Georgia Southwestern College, Middle Georgia College, South Georgia College, North Georgia College, and West Georgia College. The three black institutions in the state had not been accredited, so they were unaf-

---

[13] Novotny, *This Georgia Rising*, 81–82.
[14] *The Colonnade* (October 24, 1941).

fected.[15] The board of regents consistently ignored the needs of the state's black institutions at all levels until the 1960s.[16] The loss of accreditation meant that degrees from these institutions "would not be recognized outside Georgia."[17] The SACSS investigative committee reported that they were "convinced that the charges preferred [*sic*] against Dean Cocking and President Pittman were either spurious or entirely unsupported by the evidence." The loss of accreditation was to go into effect September 1, 1942.[18]

On December 7, 1941, three days after the SACSS announcement that ten USG institutions would lose their accreditation, the Imperial Japanese Navy Air Service attacked Pearl Harbor, and the United States entered World War II. The loss of accreditation and the preoccupation with the war took attention away from the race reform efforts of the YWCA. It was a time of disruption for students across Georgia, many of whom would volunteer for war service. In March of 1942, President Wells wrote Sandy Beaver about the loss of accreditation and concluded, "We have had a most difficult school year—so many problems—war, uneasiness, fear, distrust."[19] A GSCW student remarked about her senior year, 1940–1941, that she "had the feeling of impending calamity, and so did many others. We'd go

---

[15] The Southern Association of Colleges and Schools had begun accrediting historically black colleges in 1930. See Lovett, *The Civil Rights Movement in Tennessee*, 5.

[16] Fincher, *Historical Development*, 19. Fincher also noted that without the help of the Rosenwald Fund, Fort Valley State College would have never been possible. Through the help of the Rosenwald Fund, it was merged with Fort Valley High and Industrial School to become a four-year institution.

[17] Hair et al., *A Centennial History*, 203.

[18] Novotny, *This Georgia Rising*, 95.

[19] President Wells to Sandy Beaver, March 17, 1942, Office of the President, Guy H. Wells, 1942–1943, box 2, folder "Board of Regents-March 1942," Special Collections, Georgia College.

to dances, and they'd play songs from the first World War. We felt like something was hanging in the air, hanging over our lives."[20]

Probably the largest disruption the war caused at GSCW was the presence of 15,000 women who trained on campus from January of 1943 to May of 1945 as part of the Women's Auxiliary Volunteer Enlisted Service. GSCW was one of four campuses across the country selected as a site for WAVES training, and they greeted Emily Cottingham when she arrived as the new resident secretary in 1943. "They marched everywhere they went," said Hazel Milby Langford, who graduated from GSCW in 1946, "and they sang."[21] Marion Barber, who graduated in 1947, remembered how some of the male WAVES instructors helped cast men in some of the campus plays. Barber remembered rolling bandages to be sent overseas as well as writing letters to soldiers: "We'd get our friends to write to [soldiers] and sometimes they'd get six or eight loads from—mailed out on the same day—from people they didn't know. So everybody would sit around and write letters to them."[22] The Home Economics Department planted a victory garden, recalled Langford, from which she once gathered corn. Barber and Langford, like many GSCW students, saw their efforts and sacrifices as part of a nationwide unified front in support of the war.[23] Lewis wrote an article for *The Colonnade* informing students of the library's "War Information Center," which could help them write term papers. The center provided boxes of

---

[20] Hair et al., *A Centennial History*, 207.

[21] Hazel Milby Langford (GSCW 1946 graduate), in discussion with Helen Matthews Lewis, April 30, 2006, transcript in author's possession.

[22] Marion Denoni Barber (GSCW 1947 graduate) in discussion with author and Helen Matthews Lewis, Milledgeville, GA, October 7, 2005, transcript in author's possession.

[23] Barber, discussion.

pamphlets of "enemy propaganda," the war's "effect on economic, social, and political condition," as well as "casualty lists."[24]

The GSCW students who lived in the four dorms that had
been donated to the Navy were moved to other available dorms,
where the arrangement was three or four students per room.[25]
Students endured crowded rooms and additional restrictions
that further limited their ability to travel beyond campus such as
lack of fuel for vehicles.[26] Sugar rations were also a constant re-
minder of the reality of war. Students were required to collect
their sugar ration cards at the Peabody Practice school. *The Colonnade* reported, "The present college consumption of sugar is
based on a percentage basis according to former amounts
used."[27]

Despite the anxiety created by United States involvement
in the war and the impending loss of accreditation, progressive
change was in the air. One indicator of such change was Sandy
Beaver's August 27th resignation from the board of regents as a
sign of protest to Governor Talmadge's meddling. A former
Talmadge supporter, he publicly expressed his support of Ellis
Arnall, who was about to run for governor.[28] He confided in
President Wells, "It was not easy to break with Talmadge, but
he is so utterly wrong about this University matter that there
was no other course."[29]

---

[24] Helen Matthews, "Up-to-Date Data Supplied Students by Library's
War Information Center," *The Colonnade* (February 1, 1944).

[25] Hair et al., *A Centennial History*, 215–16.

[26] Langford, discussion.

[27] *The Colonnade* (May 2, 1942).

[28] Novotny, *This Georgia Rising*, 112.

[29] Sandy Beaver to President Wells, August 31, 1942, Office of the
President, Guy H. Wells, 1942–1943, box 2, folder "Board of Regents-
August," Special Collections, Georgia College.

As promised, on September 1, 1942, SACSS suspended the accreditation of all white institutions in the university system. The loss of accreditation was likely on the minds of Georgia's voters when they elected liberal candidate Ellis Arnall for governor. On September 9, Arnall won the popular vote by 46,363 votes (Arnall received 174,757 popular votes and Governor Talmadge received 128, 394 popular votes) and the county unit vote (discussed later in the chapter) by 112 votes (Arnall received 261 county unit votes and Governor Talmadge received 149).[30] On January 12, 1943, Ellis Arnall began his first term as governor of Georgia.

In looking back over his campaign against Governor Talmadge, Arnall knew that the Cocking-Pittman controversy had given him the opportunity to defeat him. He knew he could not beat Talmadge in an election based on the hatred of blacks, as that was Talmadge's specialty and a sentiment shared by many white Georgians; he could, however, beat him if white Georgians thought that the real issue was education and not race. Historian William Anderson put it this way: "The myth was that white Georgia would be asked to choose between the Negro and education, and they voted for education. The truth was that two racists (Talmadge and Arnall) opposed each other; one identified with closing the colleges, the other with keeping them open and accredited." Anderson concluded:

> It must be remembered that Ellis Arnall promised little to blacks. What he did do was play down the black as an issue, while letting it be known that he was anti-Negro in a more quiet and polite manner than Gene [Eugene Talmadge]. He allowed white Georgians to retain their consciences; retain their comfortable hypocrisy; to vote one way and believe another; to show some compromise which they did

---

[30] Novotny, *This Georgia Rising*, 110, 116.

want to do, while knowing deep down they had lost nothing.[31]

After Governor Talmadge's defeat, President Wells exchanged letters with his colleague, liberal educator William Heard Kilpatrick. In September of 1942, Kilpatrick expressed his happiness to President Wells and also wrote that he hoped new laws would be made to ensure independence from political meddling: "I am delighted beyond words that Talmadge is defeated. It's the best outcome of a political campaign in Georgia that I ever knew. I hope now that you school people can insist on so changing the laws that never again can an evil-minded governor interfere within the university system."[32] In October, President Wells wrote to Governor Arnall: "No other election," he noted, "ever held in the State has given me so much pleasure or so deep-rooted satisfaction. For it was a very significant victory to the State and to the South."[33] Once Arnall became governor, in January of 1943, he officially removed the governor's position from the board of regents.[34] From that point forward, the board of regents was given "constitutional autonomy" that was intended to prevent interference in public colleges and universities by the state legislature or the governor.[35]

---

[31] Anderson, *The Wild Man from Sugar Creek*, 205, 211–12.

[32] William Heard Kilpatrick to President Wells, September 25, 1942, Office of the President, Guy H. Wells, 1942–1943, box 7, Special Collections, Georgia College.

[33] President Wells to Ellis Arnall, October 14, 1942, Office of the President, Guy H. Wells, 1942–1943, box 7, Special Collections, Georgia College.

[34] Cobb, *Georgia Odyssey*, 242.

[35] Dorothy Leland (tenth president of GCSU, 2004–2011), in discussion with author, June 7, 2011, Milledgeville, GA, transcript in author's possession. President Leland pointed out that there is still great state control over college affairs through funding.

"Do But Don't Tell":
The YWCA under Emily Cottingham

The year 1943 brought Ellis Arnall to the Georgia capitol and the WAVES and Resident Secretary Emily Cottingham to GSCW. President Wells wanted to openly support the YWCA, but the politics of the Peach State warranted only his secretive encouragement, even while Arnall was governor. Wells loosened his grip, which was an improvement over the late 1930s, but he never went back to his politically naïve days prior to the trip to Fort Valley. Evidence of his new strategy was the arrangement he made with Cottingham: "Do but don't tell." Under their agreement, Cottingham reinvigorated an association that had wilted somewhat primarily due to the president's ban on attendance at interracial gatherings and the years without a strong resident secretary.

A few months before President Wells hired Cottingham, he drafted a recruitment letter to a student. The draft revealed the values he held as a liberal citizen and strong YWCA supporter:

> The Y.W.C.A. is a liberal force on the campus. For years its influence has been felt for good at G.S.C.W. There have been a few times when its policies have been too radical for a state school to embrace, but any religious group that is true to its ideals is considered radical by the "scribes and Pharisees of the day." It is difficult to put new wine into old bottles, but this is the responsibility of each student who wishes to bring her thinking and action up to date. I hope that every student will become an active participant in the program of the Y. There are too few genuinely religious students in the world, and the Y will enable you to under-

stand and appreciate religion at its best.[36]

Unfortunately, the final version did not include his praise of the YWCA. In the final version, he briefly explained the liberal arts and vocational curriculum at GSCW and encouraged the prospective student to respond with any questions she might have. It appeared that in his heart of hearts, he believed in the YWCA's race reform work. But because the excerpt above was not included in the final version, it seems that President Wells, early on in Governor Arnall's tenure, was not quite ready to fully and openly support the YWCA. He lifted the ban on attendance at interracial meetings but told Cottingham if they attended to keep it from him.

Emily Cottingham grew up in Douglas, Georgia, and had been active in the YWCA at Wesleyan College in Macon; Duke University in Durham, North Carolina; and the University of North Carolina at Chapel Hill, where she received a master's degree in social work. She had been heavily involved in interracial meetings and conferences and informed President Wells that she would like to continue her participation in these meetings and take students along. Cottingham explained President Wells's response: "I said, 'I want these girls to experience getting to meet black students who come from good families and they don't scrub other people's floors and that they are college students, too....' I

---

[36] President Wells to Pauline Trulove, April 8, 1943, Office of the President, Guy H. Wells, 1942–1943, box 7, folder "XYZ," Special Collections, Georgia College. Appearing behind the letter in the file is a sheet of paper with two paragraphs. These are the paragraphs about the YWCA. The paragraphs appear in the same font, as if typed at the same time. However, there is no date and no closing. The two paragraphs that appear to be part of the letter that was mailed explain the liberal arts curriculum and mention the vocational curriculum as well. Trulove was a student at Young Harris, and President Wells was trying to recruit her to GSCW. The author believes that the portion of the letter that praises the YWCA was never mailed.

said, 'I want to take these students to these conferences,' and he said, 'I want you to, very much. But I cannot give you my blessing. [If] you're going to have to do it—do it, just don't let me know about it, and don't let the board that governs this college know about it. Just keep it quiet.' So I did."[37]

Cottingham took students to integrated conferences at Paine College in Augusta and Atlanta University, both black institutions. Helen Matthews Lewis described a time when she went with Cottingham and other students to a YWCA conference at Atlanta University: "I spent a whole weekend at Atlanta University rooming with a black student and ended up eating in the cafeteria there and when this black woman—I came and sat down by her and she got up and moved—my roommate said [whispering], 'Oh, I'm sorry, she's prejudiced.' And I thought, 'Wow!' It's just not whites that can be prejudiced against blacks, blacks can be prejudiced against whites. It did sort of open up that."[38]

Janet Fowler also attended conferences at Paine College while Cottingham was the YWCA resident secretary. She roomed with Rebecca Slater, an African American student from Milledgeville whose father owned and operated Slater's Funeral Home. Fowler also went to Atlanta University for a conference: "Emily introduced us students to Atlanta University via the annual Christmas concert—five consecutive nights of standing room only."[39] Elizabeth Shreve Ryan also remembered Cotting-

---

[37] Cottingham Stuart, discussion. Cottingham's suggestion that "good" blacks don't scrub other people's floors revealed a misunderstanding of the connection between economic and racial oppression which she understood when she served as secretary, given the radical speakers she invited to campus.

[38] Helen Matthews Lewis, in discussion with author, Pawleys Island, SC, October 17, 2015.

[39] Janet Fowler to Helen Matthews Lewis, February 14, 2009, letter in author's possession.

ham's powerful influence: "The inspiration that came from people like Dr. Morgan and Emily Cottingham....[M]y eyes had been opened to the fact that...racial inequalities were going to have to be faced these days, and I felt very strongly that they were unfair."[40]

Lewis was an active member of the YWCA and was also influenced by Cottingham, who challenged her to rethink her worldview. The "Y apartment," Lewis said in a recent tribute, "was the center of wonderful discussions along with good food....There were study groups, discussions with visiting speakers and a safe space for a group of young women to question the stereotypes, Jim Crow laws, economic inequalities we had taken for granted. We changed under the gentle, loving care of Emily and the learning opportunities she provided."[41]

President Wells did not praise or support the YWCA's race reform efforts publicly, but he allowed Cottingham to arrange whatever events she saw fit so as to encourage white students to unlearn what they had learned about race. Cottingham's husband-to-be, Bob Stuart, lived in Milledgeville while she worked as resident secretary. He moved to Milledgeville after his service in the war. He met Cottingham at a YWCA-YMCA summer conference at Blue Ridge Assembly where they were both inspired to work for racial equality. He was employed at the Blue Ridge Assembly two summers, from 1939 to 1941. In a 2007 interview, Stuart talked about how and why the experiences there developed activist students:

> What we were experiencing there [were] the issues of the times: racism, economic depression, jobs, sharecropping.

---

[40] Shreve Ryan, discussion.

[41] Jeff Sturgeon, "Blacksburg Civic Leader Dies at 90," *Roanoke Times* (June 14, 2011), https://www.roanoke.com/news/blacksburg-civic-leader-dies-at/article_471898c1-281e-5bb4-95b5-2ae0fc38d74c.html.

The South was the nation's number one economic problem...and we had basically religious speakers and economic
speakers together in the same ethos.... [T]he Great Depression affected everything so that the student YMs and YWs
were caught up in the same situation—the Great Depression and what did it mean for religion.[42]

While Stuart lived in Milledgeville, President Wells helped
him find a job. In addition to his gratitude for helping him find
a job at the Peabody Demonstration School, Stuart appreciated
and was impressed by the risk President Wells took: "I liked the
way that Emily was able to do the things that she's telling you
about and to know that that's what he wanted her to be doing
and that he was risking his job. Even though he had made that
arrangement [take students to interracial meetings, keep it qui-
et], he was still risking his job."[43]

Cottingham brought radical Southern preachers to campus
as guest speakers for Religious Emphasis Week. Cynthia Mallory, Cottingham's predecessor, initiated Religious Emphasis
Week in 1940, and it was held annually until at least 1950. Of
all the extracurricular events available on campus, Religious
Emphasis Week and the Institute of Human Relations were the
most effective in providing students access to liberal and radical
politics and speakers. Cottingham invited to campus Charlie
Jones, Clarence Jordan, and Scotty Cowan, all of whom were
part of what David Chappell called a "neo-Populist tradition

---

[42] Bob Stuart (husband of Emily Cottingham), in discussion with author and Helen Matthews Lewis, Blacksburg, VA, December 17, 2007,
transcript in author's possession.

[43] Stuart, discussion. Bob spent his career in urban planning and is a retired professor from Virginia Polytechnic Institute and State University. In
the 1950s he worked for the Metropolitan Planning Commission in Atlanta.
He worked closely with Mayor Hartsfield, the NAACP, and the Urban
League on neighborhood segregation issues.

that centered in collective farm and labor organizations...[and] overlapped with Christian socialists and Christian radicals, influenced especially by Reinhold Niebuhr."[44]

In October of 1943, during her first year at GSCW, Cottingham invited Charlie Jones to speak during Religious Emphasis Week.[45] Jones was forced to retire from the Presbyterian Church in Chapel Hill for bringing together black and white students for meals on the campus of the University of North Carolina.[46] He studied at Union Theological Seminary,[47] as did many of the YWCA guest speakers.

World War II saw the United States imprison its own citizens in internment camps, and this was on Cottingham's mind. She invited a young Japanese man who was imprisoned in the camps in California who spoke to students about his experience and about how the camps were a violation of the rights of Japanese people. "I really held my breath about this one," Cottingham recalled. "I was so afraid he would not be accepted, but he was a charming young man and nice-looking, and those two things won him over to everybody."[48] Cottingham also arranged for him to speak with students at local public schools.

Unlike 1944, the year 1945 was the busiest for YWCA speakers since Cottingham arrived. In February, Sherwood Eddy spoke on Russia and the "Present Day World Crisis" at two YWCA-sponsored events in Russell Auditorium.[49] Eddy trav-

---

[44] Chappell, *Inside Agitators*, 47.

[45] Helen Hall, "Common Sense Religion Advocated by C. M. Jones," *The Colonnade* (October 5, 1943).

[46] Shreve Ryan, discussion.

[47] "Religious Emphasis Week Will Bring Carolina Pastor Here," *The Colonnade* (September 28, 1943): 1.

[48] Cottingham Stuart, discussion.

[49] "Y To Sponsor Eddy, Lecturer, On Present Day World Crisis," *The Colonnade* (January 24, 1945).

eled extensively and spent fifteen years in India with the YMCA. He graduated from Yale College in 1891 and afterwards studied at Union Theological Seminary. He was also an active member in the Student Volunteer Movement[50] and supported many Southern radical organizations such as Myles Horton's (and others) Highlander Folk School.[51]

In February, Clarence Jordan spoke during the YWCA's "Racial Justice Month." Recall that Jordan's version of "The Good Samaritan" was what radicalized Lewis. Jordan was born in Talbotton, Georgia, and graduated from UGA, where he studied agriculture[52] and served as president of the student YMCA.[53] He attended the Southern Baptist Theological Seminary in Louisville, Kentucky, and from there received a PhD in the Greek New Testament.[54] As a progressive Baptist preacher, Jordan started an integrated farm, Koinonia, in Americus, Georgia, in 1942, and in the 1950s was terrorized by the Ku Klux Klan who, among other criminal acts, shot into houses located on the farm with machine guns.[55]

In his February talk, Jordan "Denounce[d]...Racial Superiority," as the title of *The Colonnade* article indicated, and said: "There is no such thing as a superior race." "Mr. Jordan ex-

---

[50] Wikipedia, "Sherwood Eddy," accessed July 31, 2018, https://en.wikipedia.org/wiki/Sherwood_Eddy.

[51] Egerton, *Speak Now Against the Day*, 158.

[52] K'Meyer, *Interracialism and Christian Community*, 25, 27.

[53] E. L. Secrest to President Beeson, August 16, 1933, Office of the President, J. Luther Beeson, box 7, folder 1, "YWCA of GSCW 1928–1933," Special Collections, Georgia College. Secrest, director of Voluntary Religious Associations at UGA, typed letter on letterhead stationery that listed Clarence L. Jordan as president of the student YMCA.

[54] "About" page and "History, Clarence Jordan" page, the website for Koinonia Farm, accessed February 27, 2020, https://www.koinoniafarm.org/clarence-jordan/.

[55] K'Meyer, *Interracialism and Christian Community*, 29, 87.

plained," *The Colonnade* reported, "that there were more simi-
larities than difference between nations and races. He also
pointed out that that [*sic*] the eyes of the world are on America,
and the stand that the United States will take in the racial situation."[56]

On the same day Clarence Jordan spoke at GSCW, February 5, 1945, Governor Arnall signed into law the bill that abolished the poll tax.[57] Historian Bobby L. Lovett noted that as a
result of the poll tax, it was only about 17 to 30 percent of eligi-
ble voters who controlled elections throughout the South.[58] This
allowed Southern Democrats to be elected with a significantly
smaller number of votes compared to tax-free states. For example, in 1941, "the Georgian who chaired the House Rules
Committee had been elected by only 5,187 voters, while a
Washington State congressman represented 147,061 voters."[59]
In addition to abolishing the poll tax, in 1943 Arnall also passed
legislation that lowered the voting age from twenty-one years of
age to eighteen. Georgia was the first state in the country to do
so.

Despite progressive legislation passed under Governor Arnall's leadership, President Wells continued to provide only silent support of Cottingham and the YWCA. But under her
leadership, students flourished in their questioning of the racial
and class status quo. They created "interest groups" or discussion groups, each with a designated leader. The groups formed
around topics such as race relations, labor, current affairs, and
social projects and reflected the tradition set by Polly Moss,

---

[56] "Jordan Denounces Racial Superiority," *The Colonnade* (February 7, 1945).

[57] Novotny, *This Georgia Rising*, 150.

[58] Lovett, *The Civil Rights Movement in Tennessee*, 234.

[59] Gilmore, *Defying Dixie*, 337–38.

Margaret Kansas Smith, and Jane Cassels. Lewis served as the leader for the race relations group. The YWCA race relations and labor interest groups no doubt had a hand in bringing to campus Lucy Randolph Mason from the Congress of Industrial Organizations (CIO) and Socialist Frank McCallister of the Southern Workers Defense League in the spring of 1945.[60]

Mason was a leading advocate in the South for labor organizing. Before her position as Southern organizer with the CIO,[61] she worked with the Richmond, Virginia, YWCA as its industrial secretary from 1914 to 1918 and again from 1923 until 1932.[62] Mason was not a Communist but had no qualms about working with Communists for the cause of justice. Mason was "highly regarded by the most liberal forces in the South," Gilmore noted, and "had Eleanor's ear and a fast track to Franklin."[63] Mason was the only woman on the all-white committee that President Roosevelt commissioned to write a report on problems facing the South. In fact, releasing the sixty-four-page *Report on Economic Conditions of the South* was the purpose of the Southern Conference for Human Welfare. Both McCallister and Mason attended the SCHW inaugural conference in Birmingham on November 20, 1938, that President Wells, Mack Swearingen of the history department, and YWCA President Jernigan also attended. Journalist John Egerton noted that some people have even "credited McCallister with devising the strategy by which Georgia's reform governor, Ellis Arnall, rescued his state from the grip of anti-black terrorist groups."[64]

---

[60] Egerton, *Speak Now Against the Day*, 187.

[61] Gilmore, *Defying Dixie*, 232.

[62] Wikipedia, "Lucy Randolph Mason," accessed July 31, 2018, https://en.wikipedia.org/wiki/Lucy_Randolph_Mason.

[63] Gilmore, *Defying Dixie*, 233.

[64] Egerton, *Speak Now Against the Day*, 181, 186–87, 289.

The CIO was regularly under suspicion of supporting Communism, and Mason's and McCallister's visit did not go unnoticed by one vocal Milledgeville resident. After their campus visit, an editorial appeared in the Milledgeville *Union-Recorder* titled "No Time For Disunity." The author claimed that the YWCA at GSCW promoted "un-American doctrines." McCallister, the author said, sowed the "seed of distrust and disunity in the immature minds of the students," and that the "college will do well to purge, if necessary, its ranks of pacifists, *communists*, and isolationists if is [*sic*] to hold its place as a progressive, influential institution. This element led us into this war and we cannot afford to tolerate their subversive activities again."[65] Lewis and the outgoing president of the College Government Association, Betty Boyd, replied: "We feel that it is a wholesome thing to get diversified viewpoints on questions, so that the students can draw their own conclusions on controversial matters."[66]

Lewis also had experience in the YWCA's Students-in-Industry program. In the summer of 1945, June 26 through August 27, she and another GSCW student participated in the program:

> Marion Bessant and I went to Hartford, Connecticut on a Greyhound bus. (The trip took three days). We lived as a group in a co-op house at Hartford Theological Seminary. Among the group were a young black man from Harvard and a Japanese-American man, a student at MIT, who had been in the internment camps with his family from California. We all had to find jobs in industry, and then at night we had speakers from labor unions and social service agencies talk to us about social and economic issues. Both the

---

[65] *Union-Recorder*, May 10, 1945. Emphasis added.
[66] Lewis, "GSCW in the 1940s," 51.

black student from Harvard and the Japanese-American student had great difficulty finding work. The black man worked in an iron foundry at very hard labor, and Yoshira Befu was finally employed by a Quaker family to do garden work. (We were there on VE day.) For Mackie [Marion Bessant] and me this was the first trip North, and we discovered that we talked funny and were thought to be ignorant because of our accents and expected to be racist. The parents of the young black man from Harvard didn't want him to participate when they heard there would be two young white women from Georgia. They were afraid we would mistreat their son. To their astonishment we became the best of friends.[67]

Lewis's classmate Janet Fowler also participated in a Students-in-Industry program. Her work was in Chicago. She and her roommate, Lucy, from the University of Illinois, Urbana-Champaign, found jobs making Motorola radios. Fowler's job was wiring: "I made five wire connections in each radio unit as it was passed to me. I would reach for the unit, put in my connections, and push it along the line with my left hand—all unbroken rhythm. All on this line were female, majority of whom [were] full blooded Italians—some Polish." She explained that "on our job application we had previously been warned to list our educations as only high school graduates as employers were wary of college 'trouble maker' students." She continued, "When some of our fellow students were out on strike seeking unionization they were supported from 'the kitty.' Each week we placed 5% of our wages in said kitty in contemplation of striking students needing monetary as well as moral support."[68]

---

[67] Ibid., 52.

[68] Janet Fowler to Helen Matthews Lewis, February 14, 2009, letter in author's possession.

World War II had ended, but Cottingham kept to a busy schedule. After Lewis's and Fowler's summer experience in the Students-in-Industry program, in October Cottingham invited Scotty Cowan to speak during Religious Emphasis Week. Cowan was a Presbyterian minister who was forced to leave his church in Chattanooga, Tennessee, because of his support of striking workers.[69] When he spoke to students in 1945, Cowan was associated with the Norris Religious Fellowship in Tennessee. Lewis summed up his visit during Religious Emphasis Week:

> In his fascinating Scottish brogue, Scotty Cowan spoke to us each evening on such topics as "Religion and You in the World Crisis."... He also suggests as a means of keeping us broadminded to visit churches of other faiths than our own. Indeed, it will be a long time before we forget the well composed, thought arousing messages of Dr. Horne or Scotty's fiery challenges to our complacent attitude toward participation in the forces around us.[70]

About three months after Cowan's visit, Cottingham invited Clarence Jordan for a return visit to GSCW on January 14, 1946.[71]

Also in 1946, Lewis's senior year, she and other Georgia students ran an active campaign in support of the progressive candidate for governor, James V. Carmichael:

> Because 18-year-olds were allowed to vote in Georgia (Georgia was the only state to allow this.), we became very active in politics. We formed a League of Women Voters group, the first for young women voters. We were strong

---

[69] Dunbar, *Against the Grain*, 74–75.

[70] *The Colonnade* (October 24, 1945).

[71] "Jordan Speaks at Chapel, January 14," *The Colonnade* (January 22, 1946): 3.

Ellis Arnall supporters, and because he was not able to suc-
ceed himself as governor, the progressive candidate in 1946
was Jimmy Carmichael. He ran against Eugene Talmadge
and Ed Rivers. We formed a political campaign group
called Student League for Good Government in Georgia.[72]

Similar student leagues were formed at other Georgia colleges to support Carmichael. In a rally and straw vote, there was
a 95 percent vote at GSCW for Carmichael.[73]

On the same day as the straw vote, Carmichael addressed
students at Russell Auditorium and received a "warm, enthusiastic reception."[74] The Student League for Good Government
sponsored Carmichael's campus visit, and Lewis introduced
him. *The Colonnade* published the straw vote results of students
at several institutions of higher education around the state, including GSCW, and at each place Carmichael won big. At
GSCW, with about 80 percent of students voting, he won 95
percent of the vote. At Agnes Scott College, he won 98 percent
of the vote, at UGA he won 85 percent of the vote, and at Mercer University he won 74 percent of the vote.[75]

After Lewis graduated from GSCW in the spring of 1946,
she and other Georgia students continued working on the Carmichael campaign. Their work won national recognition and
was covered in the *New York Times*.[76]

---

[72] Lewis, "GSCW in the 1940s," 52-53.

[73] Ibib.

[74] "Carmichael Wins in Straw Vote," *The Colonnade* (June 5, 1946): 1. There
are several articles in the *The Colonnade* issue of June 5, 1946, regarding Carmichael
and the Student League for Good Government. Featured in the middle of the page is
a photo of Carmichael and a letter he wrote to the "Student League for Good Government" at GSCW thanking them for their work: "The vigor with which your group
has entered into the present fight is commendable, and will reflect credit on Georgia's
young womanhood for generations to come."

[75] "Politics with a Purpose," *The Colonnade* (June 5, 1946): 2.

[76] Beaver and Jennings, *Helen Matthews Lewis*, 28–31.

We organized students from each county to work in their home counties that summer for the candidate. George Doss of the University of Georgia and I were chosen to run the state office in the Piedmont Hotel in Atlanta as part of the Carmichael campaign, where our cause was called the Children's Campaign. We had students flying planes and dropping leaflets, three sound trucks on the road, students developing county campaigns, and vans of young people canvassing, making speeches and writing to local papers. Although Carmichael won the popular vote, he lost the election to Eugene Talmadge by the county unit vote.[77]

The county unit system was akin to the federal Electoral College. Georgia was the only state in the country to use such a system. The county unit system became law in 1917 with the Neill Primary Act and was ostensibly designed to counteract the power of urban districts because of population growth, especially in Atlanta. Yet the growing urban areas were where more blacks were residing, too, and where, in general, residents held more liberal values. In a nutshell, the county unit system was against the ideal of "one person, one vote." The system was not abolished until 1962.

Eugene Talmadge was reelected as governor. However, as he had been seriously ill for some time, it was not a total surprise when he died before he was scheduled to take office in January. Soon after his death on December 21, 1946, the "governors controversy" ensued. Herman Talmadge, Eugene's son, claimed that he was the legitimate governor, while the lieutenant governor, Melvin Thompson, claimed he was the legitimate governor, and at the same time, former governor Ellis Arnall claimed he was the rightful governor. The Georgia Assembly appointed Herman Talmadge as governor, and he served for

---

[77] Lewis, "GSCW in the 1940s," 52–53.

two months, from January 14, 1947, to March 18, 1947. Then the Georgia Supreme Court decided that the legislature had acted unconstitutionally and appointed Lieutenant Governor Melvin Thompson as governor until a special election could be held in November of 1948. Thompson served as governor from March 18, 1947, to November 17, 1948.

During the tumultuous politics of the state of Georgia during the 1940s, President Wells supported the YWCA and students' attendance at integrated conferences, albeit behind the scenes. By this time, he had earned a particular kind of reputation. Roy Harris, a member of the board of regents and House Speaker of the state, reportedly said of President Wells: "If ever there was a traitor to the white people of Georgia, it is Guy Wells."[78]

Harris was a powerful Georgia politician and loyal to the Talmadge dynasty. Appointed by Governor Herman Talmadge, he served as a member of the board of regents from 1951 to 1958 and again from 1960 to 1974. He also served as House Speaker of the state from 1937 to 1940 and again from 1943 to 1946.[79] He founded the "Cracker Party a militantly anti-black political group."[80] Harris used the county unit system to convince whites that without it classrooms and presumably other public spaces would be integrated.[81] In campaign ads for the gubernatorial primary appearing in the *Atlanta Constitution*, Herman Talmadge appealed to white voters: "A Vote for Talmadge September 8 Is a Vote to Preserve the County Unit System, to

---

[78] Hair et al., *A Centennial History*, 245.

[79] New Georgia Encyclopedia, "Roy V. Harris," last modified January 10, 2014, https://www.georgiaencyclopedia.org/articles/history-archaeology/roy-v-harris-1895-1985

[80] Egerton, *Speak Now Against the Day*, 382.

[81] Novotny, *This Georgia Rising*, 25n84.

Oppose the Civil Rights Program, [and] to Curb Bloc Voting in Georgia."[82]

Despite Herman Talmadge's running an intimidating platform of white supremacy similar to his father's (or perhaps because of), African American voters turned out in large numbers to vote in the primary, despite waiting for hours at local precincts and being purged from voter lists in some counties at the last minute.[83] After winning in the primary and the November 2, 1948, special election, Herman Talmadge was reelected to a full-term in 1950 and served as governor until January 1955. In 1956 he was elected to the United States Senate and served as a senator until Mack Mattingly defeated him in 1980.[84]

Cottingham left Georgia before Herman Talmadge became governor (the second time). In 1947, she and her husband, Bob, moved to Chapel Hill for him to attend graduate school at the University of North Carolina. After Cottingham left for North Carolina, President Wells hired Louise "Bebe" Davis as her replacement. Due to a medical emergency, Davis was unable to begin her appointment as resident secretary. Luckily, Janet Fowler had returned to Milledgeville and saw President Wells at a church service. Fowler had been accepted into the master's in history program at Columbia University, but President Wells persuaded her to become the new resident secretary at GSCW that fall. William Ivy Hair wrote that President Wells's "powers of persuasion (when he wished to recruit someone) were phenomenal."[85] In her new position, and as Cottingham had done,

---

[82] Ibid., 298.

[83] Ibid., 302–303.

[84] New Georgia Encyclopedia, "Herman Talmadge," last modified August 1, 2019, https://www.georgiaencyclopedia.org/articles/government-politics/herman-talmadge-1913-2002.

[85] Hair et al., *A Centennial History*, 172.

Fowler organized Religious Emphasis Week and secretly took students to integrated conferences at Paine College and Atlanta University. She did as President Wells had asked Emily Cottingham to do: "Do but don't tell." Such was his more relaxed way of playing the middle during a time of progressive change.

In Chapel Hill, Cottingham supervised the North Carolina Department of Welfare. She and Bob eventually moved to Blacksburg, Virginia. There, she directed the YMCA at Virginia Polytechnic Institute and State University and Bob was hired there as a professor. Emily Cottingham Stuart retired from the YMCA in Blacksburg in 1988 and passed away in 2011 at the age of ninety.

Evidence of President Wells's Success at Playing the Middle

The openings for progressive change in Georgia as a result of the Cocking-Pittman controversy and World War II allowed President Wells to relax his grip on the YWCA. He secretly supported Emily Cottingham's extensive race reform work during the controversy and managed to avoid being ousted.

Governor Eugene Talmadge wanted to keep anyone he deemed a foreigner—anyone born outside of Georgia—from having significant political influence in Georgia.[86] Talmadge had a long list of people he considered foreigners and those detrimental to white supremacy, and at the top of his list in 1941 were white liberal administrators. President Wells was a white liberal adminstrator, and, like Dean Cocking and President Pittman, had been educated at Columbia University in New York. But Wells was born and raised in Georgia and had spent

---

[86] Bailes, "Eugene Talmadge and the Board of Regents Controversy," 414.

all of his professional life in the state. In addition, he possessed little of the refinement associated with the formally educated elite. Given Governor Talmadge's way of thinking, President Wells's birth in Georgia, his desire to live and work in Georgia, and his Southern accent (unlike Pittman, who was born in Mississippi but spoke without a Southern accent)[87] made him an insider. Not receiving Rosenwald money for the college was perhaps another reason he was successful at playing the middle and ultimately able to keep his job.

Another possible reason Governor Talmadge did not oust President Wells was that the governor knew he would call on him later, which he did in relation to the employment of Sylla Hamilton. Dean Cocking fired Hamilton from her job at the Practice School, which is perhaps why she accused him of supporting integration. Perhaps Governor Talmadge knew he would eventually ask President Wells to hire her, and if he ousted him, his plan would have been more difficult to carry out.

But perhaps more than all these conditions, the circumstance that most tipped the scales in President Wells's favor was that he was more politically astute than either Dean Cocking or President Pittman. President Wells himself saw Pittman as someone who had "innate honesty" but needed to better understand the "political angles to his job." Once Pittman was reinstated as president of GTC in January of 1943, President Wells wrote board of regents member J. L. Renfroe, a Statesboro attorney, and asked him to help Pittman and to help maintain the limitations that SACSS had placed on Talmadge's power over public higher education in Georgia: "I hope that you can handle the situation there in such a way as not to give the Talmadge group a toe-hold to overthrow everything four years hence. I am

---

[87] Altman, "Marvin S. Pittman," 86.

162

for Pittman, as you know, but such men as you must help him to see that there are political angles to his job, even if he himself is not and should not be a politician."[88] In another letter to Renfroe, surprisingly, President Wells sided with Governor Talmadge in condemning Yankees: "I did not have reference in my last letter to you to the John DeLoach matter, but rather to the bringing to the state of too many Yankees, as you mentioned."[89] President Wells knew well the political angles to his job, and perhaps more than any other factor, his political skills saved him from losing it.

Over time, Howell Cone and William Heard Kilpatrick mentored President Wells and helped him develop his political skills. Cone was a politician and Kilpatrick an educator, both fitting individuals for a highly effective mentoring team. President Wells's correspondence with Cone tapered off during the war, but Kilpatrick's increased. Kilpatrick was also a frequent visitor to campus. At the time, Kilpatrick served as professor emeritus of educational philosophy at Teachers College, Columbia University, and spoke to the GSCW student body on many occasions and also addressed the faculty of the Peabody Laboratory School.[90] Kilpatrick spoke to students about the war and about how the United States, for all its proclamations of

---

[88] President Wells to J. L. Renfroe, January 29, 1943, Office of the President, Guy H. Wells, 1942–1943, box 6, folder "Board of Regents-January," Special Collections, Georgia College.

[89] President Wells to J. L. Renfroe, February 5, 1943, Office of the President, Guy H. Wells, 1942–1943, box 6, folder "Board of Regents-February," Special Collections, Georgia College.

[90] John Lounsbury, "William Heard Kilpatrick: Education Philosopher and Master Teacher: 1871–1965," 3, n.d., in author's possession. The following note appeared at the end of the article: "This article, prepared by John Lounsbury, drew much of its content from the book, *And There Were Giants in the Land: The Life of William Heard Kilpatrick*, by John Beineke, (1998), New York: Peter Lang."

being democratic, was a country characterized by profound injustice. He critiqued United States isolationism and admonished students to address these social problems in their lives beyond graduation.

With the encouragement of Cone and Kilpatrick, President Wells in some ways grew bolder. He did not openly and fully support the YWCA's race reform work, but he allowed the chapter to flourish under Cottingham's leadership. The Cocking-Pittman controversy and World War II helped create a political setting within which Eugene Talmadge could be defeated and President Wells could relax his grip on the YWCA.

Chapter 6

Lesson Four: Stay Left When It's Safe

The safe space between the Talmadges energized President Wells. For this reason and others he was motivated to hold steady on the left. At the end of the 1940s, the student YWCA was in decline, and overall there was less scrutiny of the YWCA from elected officials, judges, the American Legion, and the board of regents. In addition, there was more support for race reform from white members of the Milledgeville community; that support emerged, however, only after a rash of Ku Klux Klan cross-burnings. The final reason it was safe for President Wells to hold steady on the left was that he was close to retirement.

Response to the Ku Klux Klan
in and around Milledgeville

Emily Cottingham's successor, Janet Fowler (1947–1950), had served as resident secretary for one year when there began a wave of Ku Klux Klan intimidation and violence revolving around state elections and a meeting of the University System Council. On August 12, 1948, the Klan's Imperial Wizard, Samuel Green, burned a cross in front of the Baldwin County Courthouse in Milledgeville while more than 500 members of the Klan and inquisitive others watched. At the rally, Green announced the Klan's endorsement of Herman Talmadge for governor.[1] The special election to replace Melvin Thompson, who had been appointed as governor after the "governors controversy," was to be held in November and the primary in September.

The Klan also burned crosses at the Washington County and Twiggs County courthouses, near Baldwin County. In the southeastern part of the state, the Klan burned crosses at the Emmanuel County and Johnson County courthouses.[2] In nearby Montgomery County, on September 8, twenty-eight-year-old Isaiah Nixon, an African American man, was murdered in front of his home with his wife and children nearby. He had voted in the gubernatorial primary earlier that day and urged other blacks to vote. The two white men who shot him, Jim A. Johnson and Johnnie Johnson,[3] were arrested for his murder but were acquitted by the Montgomery County Superior Court.[4] The same night as Nixon's murder, Montgomery County's NAACP president, D. V. Carter, was reportedly attacked in his home by a group of whites.[5]

In the fall of 1948, the Klan continued its intimidation rituals. On September 15, the USG began its annual two-day meeting of the University System Council, which included administrators from both black and white institutions. The meeting location rotated, and in 1948 Milledgeville was the scheduled site, with about 175 administrators present.[6] President Wells arranged for black administrators to reside in homes with

---

[1] Novotny, *This Georgia Rising*, 285.

[2] Ibid., 286–87, 289, 293.

[3] Laura Douglas-Brown, "'Buried Truths' Wins Peabody for Exploring Racially-Motivated Crimes," April 26, 2019, website for Atlanta NPR station, WABE podcast, led by Hank Klibanoff, https://www.wabe.org/buried-truths-wins-peabody-for-exploring-racially-motivated-crimes/.

[4] Novotny, *This Georgia Rising*, 303–305.

[5] Ibid., 307.

[6] Ibid., 308.

other black families and eat in black-owned restaurants. On campus, black administrators had "separate toilet facilities, separate water pitchers, and even separate vending machines."[7] During the meetings, black and white administrators sat apart from each other. Yet rumors circulated that the meeting was integrated and that the whites of the town were going to take matters into their own hands.[8]

President Wells described what happened at the USG Council meeting in a letter to Charles H. Richardson, MD, of Macon and of the Lions Club, who had expressed his support for how President Wells handled the situation. He asked for details of the incident, and the president said that "the local chief of police and the judge of the city court came to the auditorium where the general sessions were being held and told us that groups in town were very much upset, rumors having been circulated that white people and negroes [sic] were eating and sleeping together on the GSCW Campus, and that unless something was done right away, there might be violence." President Wells reported further that the three black presidents of the black colleges located in Albany, Fort Valley, and Savannah

went to the local homes where they were staying that night, agreeing to stay until the meeting was over the following day. The next morning none of them came to the meeting, and Chancellor Paty called President Aaron Brown of the Albany State College. President Brown told the Chancellor that people in cars came to the homes where they were staying, flashed lights in the houses, took their car tag numbers, and they decided it was wiser to leave town. As they were leaving town, cars followed them and harassed them for some distance.... The following morning, Thursday, there were Klan stickers on the doors of the auditorium where the

[7] Hair et al., *A Centennial History*, 228.
[8] Ibid., 228–29.

meetings were being held and on some of the office doors in the administration building of the College. On Monday night following a [five-foot-high wooden] cross was burned on the lawn of the old Executive Mansion on the college campus.[9]

President Wells and his wife, Ruby, resided in the Old Governor's Mansion, as did all college presidents from the founding of the college until 1987.[10] Years later, President Brown told of how the group of "white rowdies tried to force his Chrysler sedan off the road with their '39 Fords."[11]

President Wells publicly condemned the Klan's harassment of the black administrators and the cross-burning on the mansion lawn. The USG chancellor at the time, Raymond R. Paty, supported President Wells and advised him to go ahead with the two-day council meeting despite warnings from locals, including one from Miller R. Bell Jr., a member of the board of regents. Governor Eugene Talmadge had appointed Bell to complete the term of his father, Miller S. Bell, resident of Milledgeville and member of the GSCW Board of Directors before the USG was formed. President Wells chose to follow the advice of Chancellor Paty and not that of Miller R. Bell Jr.

President Wells saw Chancellor Paty as a trusted colleague and encouraged him to continue as chancellor despite the intimidation and terroristic acts of the Klan and, presumably, despite Sandy Beaver's request that he be removed. Beaver had written to the board members, in a letter dated August 2, that Chancellor Paty was "arrested for drunkenness on the streets of

---

[9] President Wells to Charles H. Richardson, October 2, 1948, Office of the President, Guy H. Wells, 1948–1949, A–Z, box 4, folder 5, "Race Incident (Cross Burning)," Special Collections, Georgia College.

[10] Hair et al., *A Centennial History*, 294.

[11] Ibid., 228–29.

Atlanta and kept in jail until bond was furnished by Secretary Siebert of this Board; and Chancellor Paty was later convicted and fined in the Recorder's Court and those facts were given wide publicity in the newspapers of Georgia and other states."[12] Beaver thus called for his removal. President Wells, however, encouraged him to remain as chancellor during this difficult time:

> It seems to me you were never more needed in your present post than now. It is true that we are in a storm, and it may look like the end of the world, but perhaps it is the dawn instead.... Some of us must stand erect when the bombs begin to fall. Some may have to be blown to pieces by the enemy, but after the battle may it be said that we stood up like men. We need your leadership as never before. I hope that you will stay with us.[13]

Wells, no doubt, wanted a like-minded chancellor who would support him during a public crisis. But many people, both locally and across the state, expressed their support for how Wells handled the cross-burning. Judging from newspaper editorials and letters from friends, the response to this incident was mostly outrage and accusations that the Baldwin County Ku Klux Klan was responsible. Robert A. Heinsohn, a fellow member of the Rotary Club in Thomasville, Georgia, expressed his support for President Wells: "You may rest assured the right thinking people in Georgia and the entire U.S. will back you up

---

[12] Sandy Beaver to the University System Board of Regents, August 2, 1948, Office of the President, Guy H. Wells, 1948–1949, A–Z, box 1, folder "Board of Regents-August 1948," Special Collections, Georgia College.

[13] President Wells to Raymond R. Paty, September 30, 1948, Office of the President, Guy H. Wells, 1948–1949, A–Z, box 4, folder 5, "Race Incident (Cross Burning)," Special Collections, Georgia College.

in any action you take." He concluded, "the many friends all over Georgia...are DEFINITELY RIGHT BEHIND YOU."[14]

President Wells received support from the *Atlanta Journal*, the *Union-Recorder*, civic clubs (the Rotary Club and the Lions Club), local churches (First Methodist Church of Milledgeville, First Baptist Church of Milledgeville, Sacred Heart Church of Milledgeville), and the president of Georgia State College (now Savannah State University), James A. Colston. Colston succeeded President Benjamin Hubert, whom President Wells had worked with to bring Georgia Washington Carver to campuses across the state. As an African American himself, President Colston wrote that he understood the situation well:

> We appreciate very much the position you took with regard to the incident that occurred during the meeting of the University Council at Milledgeville. We understand the situation very well and also appreciate the embarrassment that came to you. We are fully aware of the fact that there are many people of good will who do not favor such conduct but are reluctant to speak out against it.... If more people of influence are willing to take similar stands, I am sure that incidents such as the one which occurred will not take place.[15]

The *Union-Recorder* editors wrote:

> The efforts to frighten and intimidate [Dr. Guy H. Wells] are ridiculous. Dr. Wells has been in educational work for more than 40 years and more than two-thirds of that time has been in the system of higher education. He grew up in

---

[14] Robert A. Heinsohn to President Wells, September 23, 1948, Office of the President, Guy H. Wells, 1948–1949, A–Z, box 4, folder 5, "Race Incident (Cross Burning)," Special Collections, Georgia College.

[15] James A. Colston to President Wells, October 5, 1948, Office of the President, Guy H. Wells, 1948–1949, A–Z, box 4, folder "Race Incident (Cross Burning)," Special Collections, Georgia College.

Georgia, was educated and trained in Georgia, and knows Georgia's needs for better education. He has made a contribution to the University System and has brought much improvement and advancement to the college here.[16]

In addition, William Heard Kilpatrick reassured President Wells: "I am greatly shocked and troubled at the developments. I am glad to see how the papers respond. Certainly you have nothing to regret, except the misdeeds of others. Your part throughout has been exactly right."[17] GSCW faculty and alumni also wrote letters of support.

Possibly the most impassioned letter was from Edmund Perry. Perry was a professor of religion at Northwestern University in 1954 and served as the president of the American Theological Society. At the time he wrote President Wells, he was likely working on his PhD in religion at Northwestern, where he graduated in 1950. He was born in Chickamauga, Georgia, and graduated from UGA with a bachelor's in philosophy, and he also graduated from the Candler School of Theology at Emory University.[18] Perry wrote:

> I personally am bery [sic] grateful for whatever you may have done or said to invoke the Klan's contempt. I detest everything the Klan advocates and their program is, moreo-

---

[16] Novotny, *This Georgia Rising*, 309n415. Novotny referenced this September 30, 1948, *Union-Recorder* editorial, A3.

[17] William Heard Kilpatrick to President Wells, September 29, 1948, Office of the President, Guy H. Wells, 1948–1949, A–Z, box 4, folder "Race Incident (Cross Burning)," Special Collections, Georgia College.

[18] Diane Struzzi, "Edmund F. Perry, NU Religion Professor," Chicago Tribune, December 18, 1998, http://articles.chicagotribune.com/1998-12-18/news/9812180132_1_mr-perry-major-world-religions-fulbright-professor and the website for Genealogy Buff, "Northwestern University Obituaries, Edmund F. Perry" page, accessed July 29, 2018, http://www.genealogybuff.com/il/nwu/webbbs_config.pl?noframes;read=431

ver, as anti-Christian as any organized evil I know. My sincere hope is, however, that you will not lose your position in the University System for your liberal attitude. You are doing a superb job for the enlightenment of Georgia and I want your efforts to be continued.... Again let me express gratitude for your integrity and courage and for your contribution to the moral and cultural life of Georgia.[19]

In a telegram to the *Atlanta Journal*, the Baldwin County Klan No. 291 denied that they burned the cross on the mansion yard and offered a $50 reward for anyone who could prove that the Klan had any part in the cross-burning. They wrote: "The roots of our organization are like the old oak tree that dig deep into Georgia Soil....Our code is a known code—we do not lie, or try to hide behind lies and false pretenses. We are not afraid for Dr. Wells or the State of Georgia to know how we feel. Our grievance is not that Negro school teachers were at this meeting, but that Dr. Wells did not segregate them."[20]

In addition to strong public support for how President Wells handled the Ku Klux Klan intimidation at the USG Council meeting, another circumstance made it easier for President Wells to remain steady on the left, and that was the decline of the racially progressive student organization, the YWCA. This was the case for the GSCW campus chapter, the Southern region, and nationally.

---

[19] Edmund Perry to President Wells, September 25, 1948, Office of the President, Guy H. Wells, 1948–1949, A–Z, box 4, folder "Race Incident (Cross Burning)," Special Collections, Georgia College.

[20] Baldwin County Ku Klux Klan No. 291, *Atlanta Journal*, September 26, 1948, Office of the President, Guy H. Wells, 1948–1949, A–Z, box 4, folder 5, "Race Incident (Cross Burning)," Special Collections, Georgia College.

The Decline of the Student YWCA

There are conflicting opinions as to when the decline of the student YWCA in the United States began. Citing Barbara Solomon, historian Nancy Robertson noted that the decline began in 1922. In contrast, Frances Sanders Taylor reported that a clear decline did not begin until the 1930s. They agreed, however, that the decline was in full force by the late 1930s. Robertson concluded that "by the late 1930s, students represented only 4 percent of the total YW membership."[21] Taylor speculated that one reason for the decline was that students had access to a growing number of coed Christian-based organizations. She also speculated that religious-based organizations were perhaps less appealing to post-WWII students.[22]

The decline in student associations at the national level was in full swing by the late 1930s, but in the Southern region, between 1936 and 1945, the number of associations held steady. Taylor reported that there were 212 associations in the Southern region in 1928, 156 in 1936, and 157 in 1945.[23] This stability could be because students continued to have an interest in religious-based organizations, in contrast to students in other parts of the country. Another possible reason for the stability is that the South had a strong network of regional secretaries devoted to civil rights.

At GSCW, Janet Fowler was the last director of the YWCA to have the official title of "resident secretary." In 1950 President Wells hired Weylene Edwards to serve as the first director of "Voluntary Religious Activities," which was an umbrella group that housed all the religious organizations on cam-

---

[21] Robertson, *Christian Sisterhood*, 227n15.
[22] Taylor, "On the Edge of Tomorrow," 2n2.
[23] Ibid., 8n7.

pus. This structure diluted the presence of the YWCA. In the spring of 1939, President Wells banned all students from attending any interracial conferences, but in 1943 he allowed them to attend with the do-but-don't-tell proviso he arranged with Cottingham, and, presumably, Fowler. It appeared that Edwards knew of the arrangement. In 1950, three students from GSCW attended the 1950 integrated summer conference at Berea College. In Edwards's annual report to President Wells, she expressed appreciation at being able to direct the campus chapter and that she understood the position he was in and that she had tried to not make trouble for him. Edwards also reported that she believed that this organization included the "liberal" students on campus. She concluded, "We have appreciated your personal integrity and courage in permitting us to carry on some of our activities. We realize your position and have tried to avoid any jeopardization of it."[24]

In 1949, while Edwards was director, Isabel Rogers, known as "Izzie," was hired as chaplain (a new position). She then took over Edwards's role as director of Voluntary Religious Activities, which became, finally, director of "Religious Affairs." Rogers served in this capacity until 1961. She graduated from Florida State College for Women (now Florida State University) and went on to earn a master's degree in political science from the University of Virginia and a PhD in theology and ethics from Duke University. She, too, had a connection to Union Theological Seminary, like so many of the YWCA women who shaped the student YWCA and like so many of the liberal and radical speakers who addressed GSCW students. She taught at Union Theological Seminary and Presbyterian School of Christian

---

[24] Weylene Edwards, YWCA Annual Report for 1950, Office of the President, Guy H. Wells, 1949–1952, box 1, folder "Y.W.C.A. Report 1950," Special Collections, Georgia College.

Education in Richmond, Virginia. In 1986, the YWCA designated Rogers as one of "Richmond's Outstanding Women."[25]
After Rogers left GSCW in 1961, students' interest in an organization of religious activities such as the YWCA continued
to decline, and in 1970, three years after the college became co-
educational, the Georgia College YWCA requested disaffiliation.[26]

Between 1941 and 1972, the number of associations across
the country dwindled, but there was a dramatic decline between
1972 and 1982. In 1972, the total number of student associations across the country was 268, and by 1982, there were approximately fifty.[27] In 1996, there were only twenty-two student
associations that remained.[28] Today there is only one association
that is organized as part of a college or university, as was
GSCW. That association is located on the campus of Washington State University in Pullman. Although the reasons for the
national decline in the number of campus associations are not
entirely clear, vice president of member services Becky Hines
agreed with Taylor. She concluded that the decline was largely
the result of students' lack of interest in religious-based organizations.[29]

Today the most common way for students across the country to be involved in the YWCA is through a city's freestanding

---

[25] Presbyterian Church (USA) news email list, "Isabel Wood Rogers
(1924–2007), Richmond, Presbyterian educator," March 2007. Joan Browning is a member of the private list and shared her files with author.

[26] Report, "Some Statistics about the Region," 1969–1970, box 746,
folder 8, MS 324, Smith College Special Collections.

[27] Taylor, "On the Edge of Tomorrow," 2n2.

[28] "Statistical Information on Student Associations," n.d., MS324,
Smith College Special Collections. Does not include data before 1934 or
after 1996.

[29] Becky Hines, phone conversation with author, December 21, 2015.

community association with its own executive board and its own nonprofit designation. However, there are also recent efforts across the country to connect the community associations to nearby college campuses. Some examples of registered student organizations that are sponsored by their community associations include the YWCA of North Central Indiana-South Bend and the University of Notre Dame; the Lancaster, Pennsylvania, YWCA and Millersville University; and the Greater Austin YWCA and the University of Texas-Austin. [30] Yet another structure exists at the University of Illinois, Urbana-Champaign. The YWCA of the University of Illinois is a separate legal entity as a 501(c)(3) with its own executive directors and boards.[31]

President Wells Retires

As the new decade of the 1950s began, not only was the student YWCA in decline, enrollment at GSCW was as well. During the war, in 1943, student enrollment fell to 814. By the fall of 1945, it increased to 1,123, and President Wells predicted it would continue to grow and surpass all past levels of enrollment. In the fall of 1951, however, enrollment hit a new low: 626 students. After the enrollment decline of fall 1951, in 1952, enrollment climbed only slightly to 681. [32] President Wells, GSCW faculty, and other administrators, deliberated about how to attract more students and about the causes of low enrollment. They generated several possible reasons, but the one

---

[30] Hines, phone conversation.
[31] Ibid.
[32] Hair et al., *A Centennial History*, 223, 230, 233.

that carried the most weight was that GSCW had low enrollment because women increasingly preferred coed colleges.[33]

The pattern of low enrollment continued and eventually
played a role in President Wells's decision to retire. In the
1953–1954 academic year, under the leadership of Henry King
Stanford, Wells's successor at GSCW, would reach its lowest
number of enrolled students: 470.[34] This pattern, coupled with a
general fatigue from being a liberal in a conservative state during Jim Crow, compelled President Wells to consider transi-
tioning to a new form of work. In 1951, he expressed these
thoughts and feelings in a letter to Kilpatrick. It is as if his letter
was an attempt to convince himself to stay at GSCW, even
though deep down he wanted to leave. His "greatest annoyance," he explained, "is having to serve as president during a period when the forces of reaction are largely in control in our
State." He provided an example. He feared that Roy Harris was
about to be selected as the convocation speaker. "It is difficult,"
he wrote, "to maintain one's integrity and hold one's position in
the face of such overwhelming trends toward conservatism." But
just such adversity, he suggested, is "why I should stay and help
as best I can in the fight for a better day."[35] President Wells was
undoubtedly relieved when the committee selected Dr. Pierce
Harris, pastor of the First Methodist Church in Atlanta.[36] Even
though President Wells held steady on the left while Governor
Herman Talmadge and "kingmaker" Roy Harris stood in the

---

[33] Ibid., 230–36.

[34] Ibid., 242.

[35] President Wells to William Heard Kilpatrick, September 26, 1951,
Office of the President, Guy H. Wells, 1951–1952, A–Z, box 2, folder 3,
"Correspondence & William Kilpatrick," Special Collections, Georgia Col-
lege.

[36] "Graduation Set for June 10; Class Is Largest in Nine Years," *The
Colonnade* (May 28, 1951): 1, 6.

way of racial justice, it was clear that this position drained him of energy for the presidency.

President Wells had mixed feelings about what to do. His next move was, perhaps, an effort to take another middle position, a path between leaving GSCW and staying. He requested leave to work with the State Department's Point Four Program in Libya. This was not his first administrative leave for work abroad. His first leave request was when the United States military in Germany invited him to work with administrators there to revise their public education system. This request was granted, and from January through May of 1948, he worked and lived in Germany.[37]

The Point Four Program took its name from President Harry S. Truman's 1949 inaugural address wherein he announced this program, which was the fourth piece of his foreign policy plan.[38] In the Point Four program, President Wells was to direct teachers' colleges in Benghazi.[39] But he also wanted to keep his position as president of GSCW. The board of regents responded to his leave request by stating that if he wanted the position with the State Department, he would have to resign as president of GSCW, effective June 30, 1953. At the age of sixty, President Wells chose the position in Libya and was granted one-year's leave as a professor. His appointment as professor began on July 1, 1953, and ended June 30, 1954, at a salary of

---

[37] Hair et al., *A Centennial History*, 227.

[38] Wikipedia, "Point Four Education Program," last modified January 24, 2020, https://en.wikipedia.org/wiki/Point_Four_Program.

[39] President Wells to Cason J. Calloway, April 21, 1953, Office of the President, Guy H. Wells, 1952–1953, box 1, folder "Board of Regents April 1953," Special Collections, Georgia College.

$4,600.[40] The president also earned a salary from the United States government while in Libya that was higher than his annual salary as president of GSCW.[41] While in Cyrenaica, Libya, President Wells served as the director of two colleges, one for men and one for women. He also supervised all libraries in the state and all English teachers.[42]

In April of 1953, just before he received the board's decision, President Wells wrote to board of regents member Cason J. Callaway: "The international scene has interested me for a long time, because I have realized that the future of our way of life depends to a large extent on the number of friends our country is able to make among the nations of the world." He continued, "I have had a feeling that it is better to leave GSCW before those in authority want me to leave. Perhaps a new man can come here and do the work that needs to be done better than I can."[43] James C. Bonner, whom President Wells hired in 1944, said that by 1953, after a nineteen-year tenure, the president "had lost enthusiasm for the job. Much of his energy had

---

[40] L. R. Siebert to President Wells, May 8, 1953, Office of the President, Guy H. Wells, 1952–1953, box 1, folder "Board of Regents May 1953," Special Collections, Georgia College.

[41] President Wells to Cason J. Calloway, April 21, 1953, Office of the President, Guy H. Wells, 1952–1953, box 1, folder "Board of Regents April 1953," Special Collections, Georgia College.

[42] "Dear Friend," n.d., Office of the President, Guy H. Wells, 1952–1953, Special Collections, Georgia College. Appears to be a form letter in which President Wells described the history of the location and some of his daily work. It was typewritten on letterhead from the Libyan-American Technical Assistance Service, Tripoli, Libya.

[43] President Wells to Cason J. Callaway, April 21, 1953, Office of the President, Guy H. Wells, 1952–1953, box 1, folder "Board of Regents April 1953," Special Collections, Georgia College.

gone. He was not the same Guy Wells I had known ten years earlier."[44]

Playing the middle took its toll on President Wells, even though he was able to relax his grip on the YWCA. As the YWCA declined and there was more support among whites for race reform, his job became easier. But throughout his time at GSCW, his job required him to be a good politician, and though he often prided himself on this ability, it also caused inner turmoil. President Wells's legacy allows us to understand more deeply the political nature of the position of a college president, especially when the president's political values on race collide with those of the boards and state government bodies the president must answer to. Even today, public university presidents who want to see their institutions improve their civil rights profiles at a pace faster than state governments allow must somehow resolve the tension they are likely to feel between their own sense of justice and that of conservative boards and governors.

---

[44] Hair et al., *A Centennial History*, 236.

Chapter 7

Conclusion:
Maintaining "Integrity" Amidst
"Forces of Reaction":
President Guy Herbert Wells (1934–1953) and
President Dorothy Leland (2004–2011)

President Wells and President Leland, whose terms at Georgia College were separated by fifty-seven years, faced strikingly similar dilemmas. As white liberal administrators serving under conservative state governments, their professional survival required the political astuteness of playing the middle. Despite being on opposite sides of Jim Crow segregation, they both experienced inner turmoil as they tried to determine how to lead in such a way that would allow them to be true to their liberal values on race and at the same time protect their positions and enhance the institution's ability to educate all students.

Five presidents served between President Wells, the fourth president, and President Leland, the tenth: Henry King Stanford (1953–1956), Robert E. "Buzz" Lee (1956–1967), J. Whitney Bunting (1968–1981), Edwin G. Speir Jr. (1982–1997), and Rosemary DePaolo (1997–2003). Steve Dorman is the eleventh and current president (2012 to present). To my knowledge, President Wells was the only Georgia College president who felt pressure from the state to curtail, if not abolish, the activities of a racially progressive student organization. President Leland did not experience such pressure, but she had other experiences that caused her to agonize over decisions in ways similar to President Wells.

Dorothy Leland began her term as Georgia College's tenth president in January of 2004. She came to Milledgeville from Boca Raton, Florida, where she served as vice president of Florida Atlantic University's Boca Raton campus, the largest of seven campuses. Florida Atlantic is a public four-year university in the State University System of Florida.[1] Prior to serving at Florida Atlantic, President Leland received a bachelor's degree in English, a master's degree in American studies, and a PhD in philosophy, all from Purdue University in West Lafayette, Indiana.[2]

On June 7, 2011, I interviewed President Leland about her experiences at Georgia College before she left for her new position as chancellor (president) of the University of California-Merced.[3] I began the interview by asking her to read a letter President Wells wrote, mentioned briefly in chapter 6. It was September 1951, and Wells was considering resigning and had written to his friend and colleague William Heard Kilpatrick:

---

[1] "Dr. Dorothy Leland" page, Office of the Chancellor, the website for University of California, Merced, accessed February 29, 2020, https://chancellor.ucmerced.edu/about/curriculum-vitae.

[2] "Georgia College History: Dr. Dorothy Leland," Library Guide, Ina Dillard Russell Library, Georgia College, last modified January 15, 2020, https://libguides.gcsu.edu/c.php?g=21285&p=124656.

[3] Dorothy Leland (tenth president of GCSU, 2004–2011), in discussion with author, June 7, 2011, transcript in author's possession. President Leland retired from her chancellor position effective August 15, 2019. "Newsroom" page, the website for University of California-Merced, accessed March 2, 2020, https://news.ucmerced.edu/news/2019/dorothy-leland-step-down-uc-merced-chancellor.

There is something else I should like to mention which you have no doubt felt—my greatest annoyance is having to serve as president during a period when the forces of reaction are largely in control in our State. I do not see when the opposite may be true. It is difficult to maintain one's integrity and hold one's position in the face of such overwhelming trends toward conservatism, and what I consider reaction. For instance, we were almost forced to use as Convocation speaker this year, Roy Harris of Augusta, now a member of the Board of Regents and perhaps the most influential man in the present administration in the State of Georgia. If I had said what I really feel, I would have had to resign immediately....I mention these things to show how difficult it is in this position, but perhaps these are additional reasons why I should stay and help as best I can in the fight for a better day.[4]

The turmoil experienced by her predecessor resonated with President Leland. After reading the letter to herself, she responded, "I really like this sentence," and read it aloud: "It's difficult to maintain one's integrity and hold one's position in the face of such overwhelming trends towards conservatism and what I consider reaction." President Wells's remarks brought to her mind a parent who was "very, very angry" because no one officially offered a public prayer at graduation the month before.[5]

For President Wells and President Leland, graduation ceremonies held great potential for race-related controversy and provided them with ample opportunity to maintain their integrity in the face of reaction. Charles Sherrod, a famous civil

---

[4] President Wells to William Heard Kilpatrick, September 26, 1951, Office of the President, Guy H. Wells, 1951–1952, A–Z, box 2, folder 3, "Correspondence & William Kilpatrick," Special Collections, Georgia College.

[5] Leland, discussion.

rights leader in the Albany Movement in Georgia, spoke at President Leland's final GC commencement. Sherrod began his speech highlighting the difficulties of integrating Georgia College. In stark contrast to the 17 to 18 percent of black undergraduates who constituted the student body during the 1970s and 1980s,[6] the highest percentage to date, in 2011 black students made up less than half of those totals at only 7.8 percent[7] (the latest figure from fall 2019 is 3.0 percent black undergraduates).[8] In addition to his comments on integration, Sherrod, as a pacifist, also spoke out against war and criticized United States involvement in the war in Iraq. At that point, many in the audience booed and walked out. Over the next several months, President Leland received an "on-slaught...of the ugliest mail that you can imagine. I mean, it was ugly." She continued:

> The ruse there was that there were soldiers in the audience that had just returned from the war, and I could understand them being sensitive about hearing what appeared to be anti-war comments, but the actual letters were full of racism. They were full of racist hate. So it was a fact that those words were coming from a black man who started his speech talking about the difficulties of integrating Georgia College. That framed the reaction to his anti-war com-

---

[6] Hair et al., *A Centennial History*, 336.

[7] "10 Year Trend of Enrollment by Ethnicity/Race" page, Office of Institutional Research and Effectiveness, the website for Georgia College, last modified, May 4, 2016, https://irout.gcsu.edu/requests16/recent-6.html. Hispanic/Latino: 3.9%, American Indian or Alaska Native: 0.26%, Asian: 1.3%, Two or more races: 2.0%.

[8] "First-time Full-time Freshman by Gender, Age, Ethnicity, Registration Status..." page, Office of Institutional Research and Effectiveness, the website for Georgia College, last modified fall 2019, https://irout.gcsu.edu/infocomp17/adm-gender.html. Hispanic/Latino: 7.4%, American Indian or Alaska Native: 0.4%, Asian:1.4%, two or more races: 3.3%.

ments.... They were offended because we had a radical black man who openly said that this was once a racist institution and that the town still struggles with racial issues and then made his anti-war comments. That was the offense.[9]

President Leland identified her handling of the public outcry regarding Sherrod's commencement speech as one of the two toughest experiences she had while serving as president of Georgia College.

The response to Sherrod's speech caused President Leland to reflect deeply on her own political values and to what extent she should act on them as a college president: "I've thought a lot about the difference between street activism and administration, because I've been in both places." She concluded,

> You can't be a college president and a street activist because you won't survive as a college president...that is, to step outside the role that your boss as your board will accept you to do, so you have to find other effective—but effective in different ways, I think, to be true to your principles, and so one of the things I can do is open the space for that activism to occur. I can open the space and protect the people who may be quite vulnerable because of the positions they take.[10]

As we have shown, President Wells also reflected deeply on how best to respond to events and student activity that challenged the racial status quo, when the racial status quo occupied the capitol in Atlanta. How could he best serve two opposing sides? What role should his own political values play in how he responded to white students who acted on their new worldview that the racial status quo was unacceptable? Jim Crow segregation and economic oppression of blacks was (and is) a foundation of Georgia politics. Governors Eugene Talmadge, Eurith

---

[9] Leland, discussion.
[10] Leland, discussion Ibid.

D. Rivers, Ellis Arnall, and Herman Talmadge all supported segregation and white supremacist state policy. And when resident secretaries and students of the YWCA at GSCW moved in the opposite direction toward racial and class justice and drew negative attention to the college, President Wells had a decision to make. How could he satisfy his white supremacist bosses? How could he keep the institution financially afloat, keep his job, and at the same time support the campus YWCA leaders whose race reform efforts reflected his own liberal values?

As the book illustrates, President Wells played the middle by undermining the race reform work of the YWCA on the one hand and supporting it on the other. For example, he suggested to the chancellor that the title of the campus chapter be changed to "Religious Activities." This may have afforded them protection, but this was a demotion in the eyes of the YWCA. Then he countered with a liberal move more supportive of the YWCA by, for example, taking the YWCA president along to the left-leaning Southern Conference for Human Welfare gathering in Birmingham and allowing liberal and radical speakers on campus. President Leland weighed in on his efforts to be effective under far-right white supremacist governors and the board of regents:

> I think you can legitimately see it both as a brilliant move and a weakness. And I think that depends on the perspective that's most important to you. For those students that were just beginning to break through together, with each other, long-standing racial barriers, finding a way to keep them connected was critical. On the other hand, from the perspective of the broader education of society, of making the point and winning it, that this is intolerable and it should not be something that is acceptable in our society...then I think it could be seen as a weakness, because it was a compromise that the segregationists accepted...and I

think often those two kinds of perspectives are in tension with each other. I think that Guy Wells's responsibility, frankly, was to his students. I mean he was a university president, and that he had an obligation with respect to the welfare of young people. Did it set the struggle for social justice between blacks and whites in the South back? I don't know. It's a larger historical question that I'm incapable of answering. It certainly hasn't come very far since Guy Wells's days.[11]

By 1951, President Wells was weary of managing the tension President Leland identified. He was tired of playing the middle and tired of the constant struggle to figure out how to "improve the social order in the face of people who differ with you or wish to maintain the status quo." He confided this to Chancellor Weltner in 1935, soon after Polly Moss and the YWCA students took the trip to Fort Valley that cost Moss her job.[12] President Leland understood the personal toll of President Wells's middle position and how, after seventeen years, he might question whether he should continue to "fight for a better day" or move on to other work. For President Leland, "part of the answer to that question is can I still be effective and can one individually, personally take it. You know, take what is sometimes a health issue, sometimes it's a fatigue issue, sometimes it's a—I think people who are real fighters sometimes have to step out and regain their composure and sense of strength, wherever they get it from, and then step back in. But yeah, so that's really something I've thought about a lot."[13] For college

---

[11] Leland, discussion Ibid.

[12] President Wells to Chancellor Philip Weltner, March 2, 1935, Office of the President, Guy H. Wells, 1934–1935, B–T, box 3, folder "Race Situation (Letters from Mrs. Andrews) 1935," Special Collections, Georgia College.

[13] Leland, discussion.

presidents at public institutions, whether or not one becomes a "fighter" is often dependent upon the politics of the state where one is employed.

Given the politics of the state of Georgia during each of their tenures, both President Leland and President Wells no doubt saw themselves as fighters. And they both felt the fight at a personal level. Recalling the written responses to Sherrod's commencement speech, President Leland remarked that they were "bitter and personalized so that I was held responsible because I allowed him to speak. And I even had very influential people tell me that I should consider reviewing speeches before I allowed them to be given, which in no way would I ever do, because that's—if we can't hold academic freedom sacred in an institution of higher education, there's, frankly, no hope for our country."[14]

President Leland's mindfulness and commitment to academic freedom continued at the University of California-Merced, where about 53 percent of the undergraduate population is Latinx, higher than any other institution in the ten-campus University of California system and closely reflects the demographics of the state.[15] On March 15, 2018, her article "The Power of Engaging the Other" appeared in the *Chronicle of Higher Education*. In the article she referenced the criticism she received because she allowed conservative commentator Ben Shapiro to speak on campus.[16] It is clear from our interview that

---

[14] Ibid.

[15] Jennifer Medina, "You've Heard of Berkeley. Is Merced the Future of the University of California?" *New York Times*, July 19, 2018, https://www.nytimes.com/2018/07/19/us/university-california-merced-latino-students.html.

[16] Dorothy Leland, "The Power of Engaging the Other," *Chronicle of Higher Education*, March 15, 2018, Commentary, https://www.chronicle.

her political values do not coincide with Shapiro's. Yet, for her, academic freedom meant that she must allow him to speak. She noted, "It's easier to be an advocate of something like free speech or academic freedom when you're not personally offended....So I ask myself the question, What if it was something repulsive that was morally or politically repulsive, what would my stance be, and I came to the conclusion that it would still be defending the free speech or defending the academic freedom, but also encouraging people to speak out against it."[17]

According to Joan Scott, academic freedom and freedom of speech are two different concepts. Scott, professor emerita in the School of Social Science at the Institute for Advanced Study, distinguished between academic freedom and freedom of speech. She defined freedom of speech as "the right to express one's ideas, however true or false they may be." Academic freedom, on the other hand, referred to disciplinary expertise: "a protection of faculty rights based on disciplinary competence."[18] President Leland used the terms interchangeably and made the point that even if the speech would be offensive to some it should be tolerated. The two concepts are legally separate, according to Scott, but often become intertwined on college campuses, for example, when students speak out about their right to free speech in the classroom. According to Scott and legal scholar Robert Post, whom she cites, students' free speech rights in the classroom can rightfully be curtailed in the sense that they are in the classroom to learn and the faculty member has the power to determine what is to be learned (or spoken about) based on their expertise. Even faculty rights to freedom

---

com/article/The-Power-of-Engaging-the/242833. Shapiro's first book was titled *Brainwashed: How Universities Indoctrinate America's Youth*.

[17] Leland, discussion.

[18] Scott, "On Free Speech and Academic Freedom," 1.

of speech can be curtailed in the classroom, in that they have a responsibility to focus on their discipline. In both cases, speech is appropriately limited. For our purposes, the distinction between freedom of speech and academic freedom is less important than how President Leland understood the concepts and that the controversy led to students confronting her with signs that read "Chancellor Supports Hate."[19]

President Leland stood her ground based on her understanding of and commitment to freedom of speech and academic freedom. She argued that ensuring the flow of rich debate was "*the* most important challenge that college leaders face today."[20] She concluded, "I know for certain that suppression is not the answer—it is not the path to restorative justice, and it is not the cure for the social ills that plague us." What is the path forward for President Leland? We must "move beyond yelling, denigrating, silencing, and suppression." She added, "We must provide support and healing for members of our community harmed by hate speech. But we must also find nonpunitive, noncondemnatory ways of engaging those members of our campus communities—particularly students—whose anti-Semitic, racist, sexist, or homophobic words anger and hurt others."[21]

Academic freedom and freedom of speech figured prominently in President Leland's decision regarding how to maintain her integrity and hold true to her political values when she felt pressure to do otherwise. President Wells also spoke of this

---

[19] Leland, "The Power of Engaging the Other," https://www. chronicle.com/article/The-Power-of-Engaging-the/242833.

[20] Medina, "You've Heard of Berkeley," https://www.nytimes.com/2018/07/19/us/university-california-merced-latino-students.html. Emphasis added.

[21] Ibid.

pressure, but freedom of speech did not enter into his articulation of his position until after he retired and after major civil rights legislation was passed.

After President Wells left GSCW, he prioritized his commitment to race reform and, in 1955 and 1956, traveled the state of Georgia as a member of the Georgia Council on Interracial Cooperation and spoke out in support of the integration of public schools.[22] President Wells's advocacy for integration, as a former USG institution president, was widely criticized and caught the attention of the board of regents.

On March 14, 1956, by unanimous vote (of which Roy Harris's vote was one), the board of regents revoked President Wells's emeritus status. They gave no official explanation, but it is safe to assume they revoked the honorary title because he traveled the state advocating integration. It was also around this time that the president's pension was challenged. The Georgia State Board of Education wanted to revoke his $518.93-a-month pension. Georgia governor Marvin Griffin said, "To be drawing $519 a month pension, Dr. Wells has been acting a little ugly."[23]

According to President Wells, his being a Georgia native was precisely why the state of Georgia was trying to silence him: "'The reason they're so hot on me,' Dr. Wells explains, 'is that I'm a native; I've taught their boys and girls for forty years.'" President Wells's statement appeared in the progressive national magazine the *New Republic*.[24] The author of the article criticized the campaign against President Wells and other "silent moderates" who were preachers and educators such as Chester Travelstead, who served as dean of the School of Education at the

---

[22] Hair et al., *A Centennial History*, 244.

[23] Ibid., 245.

[24] Novotny, *This Georgia Rising*, 335.

University of South Carolina and reportedly lost his job for urging that the *Brown v. Board of Education* ruling be implemented as quickly as possible. These leaders, the author believed, were part of a post-WWII generation of white leaders who questioned the racial status quo enough to help make way for the civil rights movement of the 1960s. President Wells's pension was threatened, the author concluded, because the Augusta *Courier* printed a "distorted version" of his speech at Paine College. (Roy Harris owned the *Courier*.) President Wells asserted in his speech "The Marks of an Educated Man" that an educated person had the ability to "cross national and racial boundaries." In response to the efforts of the state to revoke his pension, President Wells said, "I have nothing to retract or apologize for...I think that what happens to Guy Wells, his titles or his earned state teachers' retirement, is not the important thing, not segregation nor integration which all good men know will come in time—but *freedom of speech* and thought is the fundamental issue. If this attack upon me will help keep those rights for Georgians, the sacrifice will not be too great a price."[25]

On the same day the *New Republic* article was published, GSCW professor of philosophy George Beiswanger wrote a letter that appeared in both Atlanta and Macon newspapers protesting the attempt to deny President Wells his pension. Beiswanger argued that by threatening to revoke his pension, the Teacher Retirement Board was in danger of violating President Wells's right to freedom of speech. "The privilege to speak one's mind on public affairs without fear of reprisal is our ulti-

---

[25] "The Silent Moderates," *New Republic* (March 26, 1956): 3–4. Emphasis added.

mate defense against tyranny," he wrote.[26] Because of public outcry, the state backed down. One memorable critique of the board of regents for the revocation of President Wells's emeritus status came from the Waycross *Journal-Herald*: "This is Georgia, not Russia."[27] The point of the critique was that in the United States, unlike in Russia, citizens can speak freely and protest peaceably to address conditions of life and policies of government that citizens view as unfair. The writer condemned the board of regents because they had unlawfully punished President Wells for speaking out in support of integration.

President Wells was undoubtedly emboldened by the *Brown v. Board of Education* ruling. And in later years, as the successes of the 1960s civil rights movement set in, people all over the world were inspired to speak out against injustice. Unlike President Wells, President Leland was from a generation who had fought for rights to freedom of speech on campus. In 1964, motivated by the sit-ins and peaceful protests of students in the civil rights movement, students at the University of California-Berkeley began the free speech movement. Led by Mario Savio, students demanded they be allowed to express their political positions by, for example, staffing tables on campus that provided information to the student body.[28]

Despite their generational differences, President Wells and President Leland shared the same dilemma: President Leland described her challenge this way: "I think that if you're going to have a role like president of a university that there's certain

---

[26] George Beiswanger to the editor of the *Atlanta Journal*, March 26, 1956. Joan Browning shared her files with the authors, which she originally acquired from Special Collections, Georgia College.

[27] Hair et al., *A Centennial History*, 246.

[28] University of California-Berkeley, "Free Speech Movement 50," accessed, June 14, 2020, https://fsm.berkeley.edu/free-speech-movement-timeline/.

things you can't do and retain that role. So I think the... question is like my dilemma after reading Antigone. Am I going to engage in this heroic act and stand up for my principles and be killed by Creon, or am I going to find some other way to be true to my values and yet continue to be in my leadership position?"[29]

I believe President Wells felt similarly. For President Wells, it seemed to be a question of whether or not he should stand up to reactionary forces in state government and have the YWCA abolished or play the middle, keep the YWCA open, and thus create a space for students' progressive race politics, even if he had to occasionally force the resignation of an alum and ban student interracial activity. As President Leland put it, the dilemma is a question of operating as an administrator or an activist, and both presidents operated as administrators who found ways to play the middle.

As discussed in the introduction, playing the middle can be seen as what historian Peter Wallenstein identified as a "dual tradition of dissent."[30] He noted that this tradition was evident in Southern politics during the civil rights era, particularly among college and university presidents. Wallenstein's dual tradition characterized the leadership of both President Leland and President Wells; their soul-searching led them to "accommodate the agents of change while appeasing the forces of resistance to change."[31] President Wells's dual tradition is what we have identified in this book.

President Wells eventually moved back to Statesboro and remarried. His former wife, Ruby, had joined him in Libya during the fall of 1953, and in the spring of 1954 was diagnosed with lung cancer. After they returned to the United States, she

---

[29] Leland, discussion.
[30] Wallenstein, *Higher Education and the Civil Rights Movement*, 4.
[31] Ibid.

received treatment but died on August 28, 1954.[32] President Wells's emeritus status was restored in April of 1965, at the age of seventy-two, two months before he died. Rosa Lee Walston, chair of the Department of English and Speech, who served under President Wells and was a favorite professor of many GSCW graduates, remembered him as a "shrewd judge of personnel. But more that [sic] that he was an honest, good and humble man. He had a deep love of the school and was fundamentally an unselfish man." President Wells was buried in Memory Hill Cemetery in Milledgeville, where the three presidents who served before him, Chappell, Parks, and Beeson, are also buried.[33]

This investigation of President Wells and his response to the race reform work of the YWCA at GSCW adds another case to the growing literature on the voices of college and university presidents in the civil rights struggle. This historical account of a white, liberal college president in the Jim Crow South revealed that even though a president at a public institution occupied a powerful position, his power was limited by the state government and board members for whom he worked. However, this study also revealed that within those parameters positive change resulted. We learned that presidents can work behind the scenes to keep a progressive student organization up and running, even in the most restrictive political climate. We learned that keeping the organization open can mean that students have the opportunity to acknowledge their racial privilege, create cultures of solidarity, resist the status quo, and chip away at the powerful forces that hold racial and economic inequality in place. We learned that the progressive students of the

---

[32] Delma Presley, "A Bond Unbroken: Guy Herbert Wells after 1934," (working paper, in author's possession).

[33] Hair et al., *A Centennial History*, 172, 245–46.

GSCW YWCA were part of a small, intercollegiate, interracial movement in the South and contributed to forces for change that would later become one of the modern world's most admired and successful social movements.

Even given this positive outcome, I believe one of the costs for Georgia College of President Wells's dual tradition and skill at playing the middle was a deepening of the institution's racist structures. As President Leland said in 2011, there is not a lot of difference in the Georgia College of her day and the Georgia College of President Wells's day. In 2020, Georgia College is no longer legally racially segregated. It is, however, a "predominantly white institution." Not only is the percentage of black students low at 3 percent (with a 32 percent black/African American population in the state),[34] in 2010, Georgia College became one of five USG institutions to ban undocumented students from attending.[35] In addition, the overwhelming majority of faculty are white. We are a predominantly white institution despite the impressive gains and hard-won accomplishments of GC's first diversity action plan. GC has also instituted financial aid programs that assist first-generation students. The costs of attending, however, still exclude large numbers of high school graduates. As of fall 2020, in-state tuition and fees for Georgia College for one academic year total $9,526, which is lower than in-state tuition and fees for UGA, which total $12,080, and for Georgia Tech, which total $12,682.[36] Yet for many students, these costs put a bachelor's degree out of reach.

---

[34] United States Census Bureau, "QuickFacts, Georgia," last modified, July 1, 2019, https://www.census.gov/quickfacts/fact/table/GA,US.

[35] The other institutions are University of Georgia, Georgia Institute of Technology, Georgia State University, and Medical College of Georgia.

[36] National Center for Education Statistics, "College Navigator," accessed, June 14, 2020, https://nces.ed.gov/collegenavigator/?q=georgia+ college+%26+state+university&s=all&id=139861#expenses.,

There are many ways to fight against injustice, including a liberal university president playing the political middle in a conservative state. This book has shown how that was accomplished and has identified the costs and benefits of such a strategy. But perhaps the time for moderation has come and gone. The current response by protesters across the globe to the murder of George Floyd by white Minneapolis police officers and to the killing and murder of other black men and women by white police officers suggests that in the United States we are on the verge of making systemic change to a white supremacist criminal justice system. Over the course of a few weeks, the protests have brought about significant policy changes in some police departments. Protestors and Black Lives Matter advocates are broadening the discussion beyond the criminal justice system to include discussion about dismantling white supremacy and economic oppression in all social institutions, including education.

The COVID-19 pandemic adds to the urgency of this discussion. Indian novelist Arundhati Roy likened the pandemic to a portal. She wrote, "Historically, pandemics have forced humans to break with the past and imagine their world anew. This one is no different. It is a portal, a gateway between one world and the next." The global protests against police violence have added to the sense that we are in between two different worlds and in the process of being forced to imagine the new one. Roy continued, "We can choose to walk through it, dragging the carcasses of our prejudice and hatred, our avarice, our data banks and dead ideas, our dead rivers and smoky skies behind us. Or we can walk through lightly, with little luggage, ready to

---

https://nces.ed.gov/collegenavigator/?q=university+of+georgia&s=all&id=139959#expenses ; https://nces.ed.gov/collegenavigator/?q=georgia+tech&s=all&id=139755.

imagine another world. And ready to fight for it."[37]

In this new world, will higher education exist in its current form? Who will be enrolled? Will a college education be free? How will colleges and universities be governed? Will state governing boards be elected? As discussed in chapter 2, back in 1933, when the board of regents of the new USG arranged for an independent team to assess how best the board should govern, the team concluded that the configuration as originally created was too political because the governor served as an ex officio member of the board and because the regents represented congressional districts. Governor Ellis Arnall rectified the first problem in 1943 when he officially removed the governor's position from the board of regents. But today the governor continues to appoint the regents and fourteen out of the nineteen regents still represent the state's congressional districts.

If we define politics as a power struggle, it is doubtful that higher education in Georgia will ever become *non*-political; political parties and demographic groups will continue to struggle to be fairly represented in decision-making. But it is possible to transform the USG into a *less* political system of governance by, for example, lessening the governor's power. Such a transformation would require a fight as President Wells, President Leland, and novelist Roy suggest, and a new system would produce a new set of problems. But a less political system would ease the tension felt by liberal presidents caught in the middle between progressive- and radical-minded students and conservative state boards and governors who refuse to address the racist foundations of higher education. Dismantling institutional racism, regardless of the political positions of governors and

---

[37] Arundhati Roy, "The Pandemic is a Portal," *Financial Times* (April 3, 2020), https://www.ft.com/content/10d8f5e8-74eb-11ea-95fe-fcd274e920ca.

members of state boards, would finally mean that higher education in Georgia was no longer a site of civil rights struggle.

Appendix I

List of Institution Names and Presidents

NAMES:
Georgia Normal & Industrial College (1889–1922)
Georgia State College for Women (1922–1961)
The Woman's College of Georgia (1961–1967)
Georgia College at Milledgeville (1967–1971)
Georgia College (1971–1996)
Georgia College & State University or Georgia College (1996
to present)

PRESIDENTS:
1. J. Harris Chappell: 1889–1905
2. Marvin McTyeire Parks: 1905–1926
3. J. Luther Beeson: 1926–1934
4. Guy Herbert Wells: 1934–1953
5. Henry King Stanford: 1953–1956
6. Robert E. Lee: 1956–1967
7. J. Whitney Bunting: 1968–1981
8. Edwin G. Speir Jr.: 1982–1997
9. Rosemary DePaolo: 1997–2003
10. Dorothy Leland: 2004–2011
11. Steve Dorman: 2012 to present

Appendix II[1]

Organization of the YWCA
YWCA National Board: Founded 1906

Function: serve as the executive for the organization, coordinating the activities of all six divisions:

1. Industrial
2. Girl Reserves
3. Business and Professional
4. Student
5. Community
6. Council on Colored Work: From the 1910s to 1931 the council coordinated the work of all black members except for students.

National Student Council (NSC): Representative body elected by students at the annual National Student Assembly

Executive Committee: Advisory group of NSC representatives, national student secretaries, and staff

-----

Regional Student Councils for the following regions: elected bodies

1. Middle West (Geneva)
2. Southwest
3. Southeast (Southern)

---

[1] Taylor, "On the Edge of Tomorrow," 13. Adapted from Taylor's YWCA organizational chart.

4. Rocky Mountain
5. Pacific Northwest (Seabeck)
6. Asilomar (Western, particularly California)
7. New England
8. New York
9. Middle Atlantic

Appendix III

The Two-Tiered Summer Conference System of the Student YWCA: 1936 to 1951[1]

Year	Integrated Conference Location	Segregated Conference Location
1936	Shaw U., Raleigh, NC; not identified as cosponsored with YMCA; not identified as coed	Blue Ridge (White), Kings Mountain (Black); both identified as "joint," identified as cosponsored with YMCA
1937	Berea College, Berea, KY; identified as	Blue Ridge (W), Kings Mountain (B); both identified as cosponsored with YMCA

[1] "The Structure and Organization of the National Student YWCA Annual Regional Conferences," September 1964, reel 242, microdex 1, "History," MS324, Smith College Special Collections. Other sources used to construct this table: an email conversation on August 6, 2012, between the author and Maida Goodwin, archivist at the Sophia Smith Collection of Women's History, Smith College Special Collections; Frances Sanders Taylor's unpublished dissertation; the Southern Historical Collection at the University of North Carolina, Chapel Hill (1939 integrated conference program); and John Egerton's *Speak Now Against the Day*. The Berea College conferences are not listed as integrated for the years 1948 and 1949. However, we assume they are integrated because of the history of integrated conferences at Berea and because of the college's historical commitment to end segregation.

	"joint," meaning cosponsored with YMCA	
Year	Integrated Conference Location	Segregated Conference Location
1938	Berea College, Berea, KY; identified as cosponsored with YMCA; identified as sponsored by YWCA only in conference program, but open to men as well	Blue Ridge (W), Kings Mountain (B); both identified as cosponsored with YMCA; last Kings Mountain Conference
1939	Talladega College, Talladega, AL; identified as cosponsored with YMCA	Blue Ridge (W); identified as cosponsored with YMCA
1940	Talladega College, Talladega, AL; not identified as cosponsored with YMCA; not identified as coed	Blue Ridge (W); not identified as cosponsored with YMCA; not identified as coed
1941	Talladega College; Talladega, AL; identified as cosponsored with YMCA	Blue Ridge (W); identified as cosponsored with YMCA
Year	Integrated Con-	Segregated Conference Location

	ference Loca-tion	
1942	Talladega College; Talladega, AL; identified as cosponsored with YMCA	Blue Ridge (W); identified as cosponsored with YMCA
1943	No record of summer conference	No record of summer conference
1944	Berea College, Berea, KY, and Hampton Institute, Hampton, VA; HI conference identified as cosponsored with YMCA	Blue Ridge (W); identified as cosponsored with YMCA
1945	Camp Highland Lake, Hendersonville, NC; identified as cosponsored with YMCA in 1964 document and as interracial according to Taylor (p. 150)	WWII travel ban; no conferences of any type listed in *The Intercollegian*, monthly magazine of the National Intercollegiate Christian Confederation
1946	Camp Highland Lake, Hendersonville, NC; identified as cosponsored	Blue Ridge, open to white men only, according to *The Intercollegian*

Year	Integrated Conference Location	Segregated Conference Location
1946 cont.	with YMCA in 1964 document and as interracial according to Egerton	
1947	Berea College, Berea, KY; identified as cosponsored with YMCA. No conferences listed in 1964 document	
1948	Berea College, Berea, KY; identified as cosponsored with YMCA	No conferences listed in *The Intercollegian*, (Maida Goodwin, August 6, 2012)
1949	Berea College, Berea, KY; identified as cosponsored with YMCA; last year recorded in 1964 document	No conferences listed in *The Intercollegian*; last year recorded in 1964 document
1950	Berea College, Berea, KY; identified as cosponsored	No record of summer conference

Year	Integrated Conference Location	Segregated Conference Location
1950 cont.	with YMCA (Office of the President files, 1950, resident secretary report, Special Collections, Georgia College)	
1951	No record of summer conference	No record of summer conference

Appendix IV

Survey of White Students Conducted by the YWCA at the 1927 Blue Ridge Summer Conference, Black Mountain, NC[1]

	Yes	No	Uncertain
Q1: Southern industry is so different from industry in other sections that it does not experience the same difficulties.	101	124	59
Q2: A woman has the same right to a career as a man.	280	7	7
Q3: I am willing to admit Negroes into full citizenship.	142	88	81
Q4: Public worship in church contributes much to my spiritual life.	336	24	30
Q5: Mill hands get such high wages that they all have Fords and silk shirts.	12	247	35
Q6: We have no right to criticize the Church.	68	191	37
Q7: Welfare work answers the problems of industrial workers.	42	125	107
Q8: I am willing to admit Negroes into my intended profession as equals.	83	147	78
Q9: It is not the Church's business to participate in social and political questions.	85	154	55

---

[1] Survey, "Blue Ridge: 1927," box 2 reel 144, microdex 2 MS324, Smith College Special Collections. Some of the most provocative questions appear in bold-faced type.

	Yes	No	Uncertain
Q10: The industrial revolution has curtailed the customary activities of women, and it becomes necessary for society to re-evaluate the way its women spend their time.	189	38	64
Q11: In racial situations I am confronted with conflicting loyalties: To my family OR to a cause of human brotherhood	**111**	**98**	**45**
Q11: To the Southern Regional Council [of the YWCA] OR to my alma Mater	57	108	70
Q11: To my social status OR to my genuine interest in better racial understanding	103	72	55
Q11: To my church OR to my own understanding of Jesus	89	90	54
Q12: Public worship should have a greater effect on daily personal and social attitudes and practices.	281	3	8
Q13: The boss is the worker's best friend.	95	90	106
Q14: I am willing to admit Negroes to live on my street.	**46**	**195**	**64**
Q15: The local church should receive into its membership persons of different racial and national groups in order to fulfill its ideal of fellowship.	140	70	72
Q16: Any dutiful daughter will readily give up her own interests to remain at home with a widowed mother.	26	88	123
Q17: A labor union is a good thing for a worker.	147	19	118
Q18: Disinclination to associate across race lines in a neighborhood is due to: Possibility of losing social status	**233**	**30**	**21**
Q18: Fear of inter-marriage	226	33	14
Q18: Lack of culture on the part of Negroes	231	21	17
Q18: Different standards of morals in two groups	226	19	33

	Yes	No	Uncertain
Q18: Intellectual inferiority of the Negro	181	36	44
Q19: Through its teaching, the Church enables young people to see the moral issues involved in daily conduct.	178	45	68
Q20: The father should be the unquestioned head of the family.	40	169	85
Q21: Industrial conditions in the South are as good or better than in other sections.	63	76	148
Q22: The present segregation laws are: A protection to the Negro	74	63	107
Q22: an act of discrimination against an inferior group, making it possible for each group to develop independently of the other	95	46	106
Q23: A parent must conscientiously and progressively push the child out of the home toward complete independence of character.	94	130	62
Q24: The mill village is a good place to train children for future citizenship.	17	203	67
Q25: It seems improbable that Jesus anticipated the existence of churches called by his Name.	56	73	155
Q26: I am willing to move in the same social circles as the Negro.	22	238	39
Q27: Men and women should share equally in the initiative of finding and choosing mates.	152	86	75
Q28: The Federal Child Labor Amendment originated in Russia.	8	101	162
Q29: That something is wrong with marriage today is universally admitted.	219	34	34

Glossary

Ideology: a set of beliefs that promote or appear to promote one's own interests or the interests of one's group.

Integrated: gatherings of blacks and whites with the purpose of addressing racial inequality, and all aspects of the gathering are carried out under conditions of social equality.

Interracial: gatherings of blacks and whites with the purpose of discussing racial inequality. It is unclear if all interracial gatherings were carried out under the conditions of social equality, that is, on equal footing in all respects between black and white participants, such as sharing meals and accommodations. They were seen as threatening, however, by the white power structure because the people coming together questioned the racial status quo at varying levels.

Liberal: a set of political beliefs that reside to the left of center, wherever the center may be for a particular time frame. What's important for this study is that a liberal position included support of legal racial segregation as well as support of government efforts to improve the opportunities for education, health, and overall well-being of African American citizens. GSCW President Guy Wells is emblematic of this position as well as Governor Ellis Arnall, USG Chancellor Philip Weltner, and USG Chancellor Raymond Paty.

Progressive: a set of political beliefs that are positioned to the left of liberal beliefs. In this study "progressive" represents beliefs that oppose Jim Crow (legal) segregation. The GSCW YWCA is designated a progressive student organization because of its leaders in the South who were opposed to segregation; however, not every member of the organization opposed segregation.

Radical: a set of political beliefs that are positioned to the left of liberal beliefs. These beliefs include a commitment to systemic change and the understanding that race and economics are inter-twined, that is, that movement toward racial equity can go only so far without attention to economic oppression. Radical beliefs also include opposition to Jim Crow segregation.

Social Equality: A term used during the interwar years and up until the modern civil rights movement to refer to racial equality or racial integration. It specifically referred to integrated settings where blacks and whites interacted on equal footing in all ways. For example, both blacks and whites sat together and ate meals at the same table. In a setting of social equality there were no Jim Crow laws/rules followed, either formally or informally.

Bibliography

Altman, Pamela Frost. "Marvin S. Pittman: A Historical Inquiry of His Life, Legacy and Leadership." EdD diss., Georgia Southern University, 2007.

Anderson, William. *The Wild Man from Sugar Creek: The Political Career of Eugene Talmadge*. Baton Rouge: Louisiana State University Press, 1975.

Ashby, Warren. *Frank Porter Graham: A Southern Liberal*. Winston-Salem, NC: John F. Blair, Publisher, 1989.

Bailes, Sue. "Eugene Talmadge and the Board of Regents Controversy." *Georgia Historical Quarterly* 53/4 (1969): 409–32.

Beineke, John A. *And There Were Giants in the Land: The Life of William Heard Kilpatrick*. New York: Peter Lang International Academic Publishers, 1998.

Brown-Nagin, Tomiko. *Courage to Dissent: Atlanta and the Long History of the Civil Rights Movement*. New York: Oxford University Press, 2011.

Brundage, W. Fitzhugh. *Lynching in the New South: Georgia and Virginia, 1880–1930*. Champaign: University of Illinois Press, 1988.

Chappell, David L. *Inside Agitators: White Southerners in the Civil Rights Movement*. Baltimore, MD: Johns Hopkins University Press, 1994.

Cobb, James C. *Georgia Odyssey*. Athens: University of Georgia Press, 1997.

Cohen, Robert. *When the Old Left Was Young: Student Radicals and America's First Mass Student Movement, 1929–1941*. New York: Oxford University Press, 1993.

Cole, Eddie R. "College Presidents and Black Student Protests: A Historical Perspective on the Image of Racial Inclusion and the Reality of Exclusion." *Peabody Journal of Education* 93/1 (2018): 78–89.

Collins, Patricia Hill. *Black Feminist Thought: Knowledge, Consciousness, and the Politics of Empowerment*. New York: Routledge, 1991.

Dewey, John. *Democracy and Education: An Introduction to the Philosophy of Education*. New York: Macmillan Company, 1944.

Dunbar, Anthony P. *Against the Grain: Southern Radicals and Prophets, 1929–1959.* Charlottesville: University Press of Virginia, 1981.

Dykeman, Wilma. *Prophet of Plenty: The First Ninety Years of W. D. Weatherford.* Knoxville: University of Tennessee Press, 1966.

Egerton, John. *Speak Now Against the Day: The Generation Before the Civil Rights Movement in the South.* Chapel Hill: University of North Carolina Press, 1993.

Fass, Paula S. *The Damned and the Beautiful: American Youth in the 1920's.* New York: Oxford University Press, 1977.

Fincher, Cameron. *Historical Development of the University System of Georgia: 1932–1990.* Athens: Institute of Higher Education of the University of Georgia, 1991.

Geiger, Roger L. *The History of American Higher Education: Learning and Culture from the Founding to World War II.* Princeton, NJ: Princeton University Press, 2015.

Gilmore, Glenda Elizabeth. *Defying Dixie: The Radical Roots of Civil Rights, 1910–1950.* New York: W. W. Norton, 2008.

Gilpin, Patrick J., and Marybeth Gasman. *Charles S. Johnson: Leadership Beyond the Veil in the Age of Jim Crow.* Albany: State University of New York Press, 2003.

Gurr, Charles Stephen. *The Personal Equation: A Biography of Steadman Vincent Sanford.* Athens: University of Georgia Press, 1999.

Hair, William Ivy, James C. Bonner, Edward B. Dawson, and Robert J. Wilson III. *A Centennial History of Georgia College.* Milledgeville: Georgia College, 1979.

Hall, Jacquelyn Dowd. "Open Secrets: Memory, Imagination, and the Refashioning of Southern Identity." *American Quarterly* 50/1 (1998): 109–24.

———. *Revolt Against Chivalry: Jesse Daniel Ames and the Women's Campaign Against Lynching.* New York: Columbia University Press, 1979.

Kamp, Joseph P. *Behind the Lace Curtains of the YWCA.* New York: Constitutional Educational League, Inc., 1948.

Kelley, Robin D. G. *Hammer and Hoe: Alabama Communists During the Great Depression.* Chapel Hill: University of North Carolina Press, 1990.

K'Meyer, Tracy Elaine. *Interracialism and Christian Community in the Postwar South: The Story of Koinonia Farm.* Charlottesville: University Press of Virginia, 1997.

Lewis, Helen Matthews. "GSCW in the 1940s: Mary Flannery Was There Too." *Flannery O'Connor Review* 3 (2005): 49–58.

Lovett, Bobby L. *The Civil Rights Movement in Tennessee: A Narrative History.* Knoxville: University of Tennessee Press, 2005.

Lynn, Susan. *Progressive Women in Conservative Times: Racial Justice, Peace, and Feminism, 1945 to the 1960s.* New Brunswick, NJ: Rutgers University Press, 1992.

Newcomer, Mabel. *A Century of Higher Education for American Women.* New York: Harper & Brothers Publishers, 1959.

Nixon, Herman C. *Forty Acres and Steel Mules.* Chapel Hill: University of North Carolina Press, 1938.

Novotny, Patrick. *This Georgia Rising: Education, Civil Rights, and the Politics of Change in Georgia in the 1940s.* Macon, GA: Mercer University Press, 2007.

Presley, Delma Eugene. *The Southern Century: Georgia Southern University: 1906–2006.* Statesboro: Georgia Southern University, 2006.

Raper, Arthur F. *Preface to Peasantry: A Tale of Two Black Belt Counties.* Chapel Hill: University of North Carolina Press, 1936.

———. *The Tragedy of Lynching.* Chapel Hill: University of North Carolina Press, 1933.

Record, Jane Cassels. "Desegregation Near the Bottom of the Ladder." *Antioch Review* 16/1 (1956): 23–33.

———. "The Marine Radioman's Struggle for Status." *American Journal of Sociology* 62/4 (January 1, 1957): 353–59.

———. "The Red-Tagging of Negro Protest." *American Scholar* 26/3 (1957): 325–33.

———. "The War Labor Board: An Experiment in Wage Stabilization." *American Economic Review* 34/1 (March 1, 1944): 98–110.

Record, Jane Cassels and Wilson Record. "Ethnic Studies and Affirmative Action: Ideological Roots and Implications for the Quality of American Life." *Social Science Quarterly* 55/2 (September 1974): 502–19.

———. "Ideological Forces and the Negro Protest." *Annals of the American Academy of Political and Social Science* 357 (January 1, 1965): 89–96.

————. "Totalist and Pluralist Views of Women's Liberation: Some Reflections on the Chinese and American Settings." *Social Problems* 23/4 (April 1, 1976): 402–14.

Record, Wilson. *The Negro and the Communist Party*. New York: Atheneum, 1971.

Robertson, Nancy Marie. *Christian Sisterhood, Race Relations, and the YWCA, 1906–1946*. Urbana: University of Illinois Press, 2007.

Schultz, Mark. "Benjamin Hubert and the Association for the Advancement of Negro Country Life." In *Beyond Forty Acres and a Mule: African American Landowning Families Since Reconstruction*. Edited by Evan P. Bennett and Debra Ann Reid. Gainesville: University Press of Florida, 2012, pp. 83–105.

Scott, Joan W. "On Free Speech and Academic Freedom." *Journal of Academic Freedom* 8 (2017): https://www.aaup.org/sites/default/files/Scott_0.pdf.

Shapiro, Ben. *Brainwashed: How Universities Indoctrinate America's Youth*. Nashville: WND Books, 2004.

Smith, Gerald L. *A Black Educator in the Segregated South: Kentucky's Rufus B. Atwood*. Lexington: University Press of Kentucky, 1994.

Solomon, Barbara Miller. *In the Company of Educated Women: A History of Women and Higher Education in America*. New Haven, CT: Yale University Press, 1985.

Tanner, Daniel. *Crusade for Democracy: Progressive Education at the Crossroads*. Rev. ed. Albany: State University of New York Press, 2015.

Taylor, Frances Sanders. "'On the Edge of Tomorrow:' Southern Women, the Student YWCA, and Race, 1929–1944." PhD diss., Stanford University, 1984.

University Archives, Special Collections, Ina Dillard Russell Library, Georgia College, Milledgeville, GA.

Wallenstein, Peter. "Introduction: Higher Education, Black Access, and the Civil Rights Movement." In *Higher Education and the Civil Rights Movement: White Supremacy, Black Southerners, and College Campuses*. Edited by Peter Wallenstein. Gainesville: University Press of Florida, 2008, pp. 1–16.

Whittington, Erica L. "Interracial Dialogue and the Southern Student Human Relations Project." In *Rebellion in Black and White: Southern Student Activism in the 1960s*. Edited by Robert Cohen and David J.

Snyder. Baltimore, MD: Johns Hopkins University Press, 2013, pp. 83–105.

Williamson, Joy Ann. *Radicalizing the Ebony Tower: Black Colleges and the Black Freedom Struggle in Mississippi*. New York: Teachers College Press, 2008.

YWCA of the U.S.A. Records, Sophia Smith Collection of Women's History, Smith College Special Collections, Northampton, MA.

Index